THE BOOK

OF

PRIVATE DEVOTION.

THE BOOK

OF

PRIVATE DEVOTION,

A SERIES OF

PRAYERS AND MEDITATIONS:

WITH

AN INTRODUCTORY ESSAY ON PRAYER,

CHIEFLY FROM THE WRITINGS OF

HANNAH MORE.

REVISED AND ENLARGED.

"Enter into thy closet, and when thou hast shut thy door, pray to thy Father which is in secret."

NEW YORK:
ROBERT CARTER & BROTHERS,
285 Broadway.
1850.

CONTENTS.

DEVOUT MEDITATIONS.

DEVOTIONAL POETRY.

PRIVATE DEVOTION.

PART I.

AN INTRODUCTORY ESSAY ON PRAYER AND PRIVATE DEVOTION.

AN INTRODUCTORY

ESSAY ON PRAYER, &c.

Prayer is the application of want to Him who alone can relieve it—the confession of sin to Him who alone can pardon it. It is the urgency of poverty, the prostration of humility, the fervency of penitence, the confidence of trust. It is not eloquence, but earnestness; not the definition of helplessness, but the feeling of it: not figures of speech, but compunction of soul. It is the "Lord, save us, we perish," of drowning Peter—the cry of faith to the ear of mercy.

Adoration is the noblest employment of created beings; confession the natural language of guilty creatures; gratitude the spontaneous expression of pardoned sinners. Prayer is desire: it is not a mere conception of the mind, not an effort of the intellect, not an act of the memory, but an elevation of the soul towards its Maker; a pressing sense of our own ignorance and infirmity, a consciousness of the perfections of God, of his readiness to hear, of his power to help, of his willingness to save. It is not an emotion produced in the senses, nor an effect wrought by the imagination; but a determination of the will, an effusion of the heart.

Prayer is an act both of the understanding and of the heart. The understanding must apply itself to the knowledge of the

Divine perfections, or the heart will not be led to the adoration of them. It would not be a *reasonable* service if the mind were excluded. It must be rational worship, or the human worshipper will not bring to the service the distinguishing faculty of his nature, which is reason. It must be spiritual worship, or it will want the distinctive quality to make it acceptable to Him who is a spirit, and who has declared that he will be worshipped "in spirit and in truth."

Man is not only a sinful but also a helpless, and therefore a dependant being. This offers new and powerful motives to prayer, and shows the necessity of looking continually to a higher power, to a better strength than our own. If that Power sustains us not we fall; if He direct us not we wander. His guidance is not only perfect freedom, but perfect safety. Our greatest danger begins from the moment we imagine we are able to go alone.

He who does not believe this fundamental truth, "the helplessness of man," on which the other doctrines of the Bible are built—even he who does nominally profess to assent to it as a doctrine of Scripture, yet if he does not experimentally acknowledge it—if he does not feel it in the convictions of his own awakened conscience, in his discovery of the evil workings of his own heart, and the wrong propensities of his own nature, all bearing their testimony to its truth,—such a one will not pray earnestly for its cure—will not pray with that feeling of his own helplessness, with that sense of dependance on Divine assistance which alone makes prayer efficacious.

Nothing will make us truly humble, nothing will make us constantly vigilant, nothing will entirely lead us to have recourse to prayer, so fervently or so frequently as this ever-abiding sense of our corrupt and helpless nature, as our not being able to ascribe any disposition in ourselves to anything that is good, or any power to avoid, by our own strength, anything that is evil.

Prayer is right in itself as the most powerful means of resisting sin and advancing in holiness. It is above all right, as everything is which has the authority of Scripture, the command of God, and the example of Christ.

There is perfect consistency in all the

ordinances of God; a perfect congruity in the whole scheme of his dispensations. If man were not a corrupt creature, such prayer as the gospel enjoins would not have been necessary. Had not prayer been an important means for curing those corruptions, a God of perfect wisdom would not have ordered it. He would not have prohibited everything which tends to inflame and promote them, had they not existed; nor would he have commanded everything that has a tendency to diminish and remove them, had not their existence been fatal. Prayer, therefore, is an indispensable part of his economy and of our obedience.

We cannot attain to a just notion of prayer while we remain ignorant of our own nature, of the nature of God as revealed in Scripture, of our relations to him, and of our dependance on him. If, therefore, we do not live in the daily study of the holy Scriptures, we shall want the highest motive to this duty, and the best helps for performing it; if we do, the cogency of these motives, and the inestimable value of these helps, will render argument unnecessary, and exhortation superfluous.

One cause, therefore, of the dulness of many Christians in prayer is their slight acquaintance with the sacred volume. They hear it periodically, they read it occasionally, they are contented to know it historically, to consider it superficially; but they do not endeavor to get their minds imbued with its spirit. If they store their memory with its facts, they do not impress their hearts with its truth. They do not regard it as the nutriment on which their spiritual life and growth depend. They do not pray over it; they do not consider all its doctrines as of practical application; they do not cultivate that spiritual discernment which alone can enable them judiciously to appropriate its promises, and apply its denunciations, to their own actual case. They do not use it as an unerring line to ascertain their own rectitude, or detect their own obliquity.

Though we cannot pray with a too deep sense of sin, we may make our sins too exclusively the object of our prayers. While we keep, with a self-debasing eye, our own corruptions in view, let us look with equal intentness on that mercy which cleanseth from all sin. Let our prayers be all humiliation, but let them not be all complaint. When men indulge no other thought but that they are rebels, the hopelessness of pardon hardens them into disloyalty. Let us look to the mercy of the King as well as to the rebellion of the subject. If we contemplate his grace as displayed in the gospel, then, though our humility will increase, our despair will vanish. Gratitude in this, as in human instances, will create affection:—"We love him, because he first loved us."

Let us, therefore, always keep our unworthiness in view, to remind us that we stand in need of the mercy of God in Christ, but never plead it as a reason why we should not draw nigh to him to implore that mercy. The best men are unworthy for their own sakes; the worst, on repentance, will be accepted for His sake and through his merits.

In prayer, then, the perfections of God, and especially his mercies in our redemption, should occupy our thoughts as much as our sins; our obligations to him as much as our departures from him. We should keep up in our hearts a constant sense of our own weakness, not with a design to discourage the mind and depress the spirits, but with a view to drive us out of ourselves in search of the Divine assistance. We should contemplate our infirmity in order to draw us to look for his strength, and to seek that power from God which we vainly look for in ourselves: we do not tell a sick friend of his danger in order to grieve and terrify him, but to induce him to apply to his physician, and to have recourse to his remedy.

The success of prayer, though promised to all who offer it in perfect sincerity, is not so frequently promised to the cry of distress, to the impulse of fear, or the emergency of the moment, as to humble perseverance in devotion; it is to patient waiting, to assiduous solicitation, to unwearied importunity that God has declared that He will lend His ear, that He will give the communication of His Spirit, that He will grant the return of our requests. Nothing but this holy perseverance can keep up in our minds a humble sense of our dependance. It is not by a mere casual petition, however passionate, but by habitual application, that devout affections are excited and maintained, that our converse with Heaven is carried on. It is by no other means that we can be assured, with St. Paul, that "we are risen with Christ," but this obvious one—that we thus seek the things which are above; that the heart is renovated; that the mind is lifted above this low scene of things; that the spirit breathes in a purer atmosphere; that the whole man is enlightened, and strengthened, and purified; and that the more frequently so the more nearly we approach to the throne of God. We shall find also, that prayer not only expresses but elicits the Divine grace.

Prayer draws all the Christian graces into its focus. It draws Charity, followed by her lovely train, her forbearance with faults, her forgiveness of injuries, her pity for errors, her compassion for want. It draws Repentance, with her holy sorrows, her pious resolutions, her self-distrust. It attracts Faith, with her elevated eye—Hope, with her grasped anchor—Beneficence, with her open hand—Zeal, looking far and wide to serve—Humility, with introverted eye, looking at home. Prayer, by quickening these graces in the heart, warms them into life, fits them for service, and dismisses each to its appropriate practice. Cordial prayer is mental virtue; Christian virtue is spiritual action. The mould into which genuine prayer casts the soul is not effaced by the suspension of the act, but retains some touches of the impression till the act is repeated.

But he to whom the duty of prayer is unknown, and by whom the privilege of prayer is unfelt; or he by whom it is neglected; or he who uses it for form and not from feeling, may probably say, Will this work, wearisome even if necessary, never know an end? Will there be no period when God will dispense with its regular exercise? Will there never be such an attainment of the end proposed, as that we may be allowed to discontinue the means?

To these interrogatories there is but one answer—an answer which shall be also made by an appeal to the inquirer himself.

If there be any day in which we are quite certain that we shall meet with no trial from Providence, no temptation from the world; any day in which we shall be sure to have no wrong tempers excited in ourselves, no call to bear with those of others, no misfortune to encounter, and no need of Divine assistance to endure it; on that morning we may safely omit prayer.

If there be an evening in which we have received no protection from God, and experienced no mercy at his hands; if we have not neglected a single opportunity of doing or receiving good; if we are quite certain that we have not once spoken unadvisedly with our lips, nor entertained one vain or idle thought in our heart; on that night we may safely omit to praise God, and to confess our own sinfulness; on that night we may safely omit humiliation and thanksgiving. To repeat the converse would be superfluous.

When we can conscientiously say, that religion has given a tone to our conduct, a law to our actions, a rule to our thoughts, a bridle to our tongue, a restraint to every wrong passion, a check to every ill temper, then some will say, We may safely be dismissed from the drudgery of prayer, it will then have answered all the ends which you so tiresomely recommend. So far from it, we really figure to ourselves, that if we could hope to hear of a human being taught to such perfection of discipline, it would unquestionably be found that this would be the very being who would continue most perseveringly in the practice of that devotion which had so materially contributed to bring his heart and mind into so desirable a state, who would most tremble to discontinue prayer, who would be most appalled at the thought of the condition into which such discontinuance would be likely to reduce him. Whatever others do, he will continue forever to "sing praises unto Thee, O Thou most Highest; he will continue to tell of Thy loving-kindness early in the morning, and of thy truth in the night-season."

Our reluctant devotions may remind us of the remark of a certain great political wit, who apologized for his late attendance in Parliament by his being detained while a party of soldiers were *dragging a volunteer* to his duty. How many excuses do we find for not being in time! How many apologies for brevity! How many evasions for neglect! How unwilling, too often, are we to come into the divine presence, how reluctant to remain in it? Those hours which are least valuable for business, which are least seasonable for pleasure, we commonly give to religion. Our energies which were so exerted in the society we have just quitted, are sunk as we approach the divine presence. Our hearts, which were all alacrity in some frivolous conversation, become cold and inanimate, as if it were the natural property of devotion to freeze the affections. Our animal spirits, which so readily performed their functions before, now slacken their vigor and lose their vivacity. The sluggish body sympathizes with the unwilling mind, and each promotes the deadness of the other; both are slow in listening to the call of duty; both are soon weary in performing it. As prayer requires all the energies of the compound being of man, so we too often feel as if there were a conspiracy of body, soul, and spirit, to decline and disqualify us for it.

To be deeply impressed with a few fundamental truths, to digest them thoroughly, to meditate on them seriously, to pray over them fervently, to get them deeply rooted in the heart, will be more productive of faith and holiness than to labor after variety, ingenuity, or elegance. The indulgence of imagination will rather distract than edify. Searching after ingenious thoughts will rather divert the attention from God to ourselves, than promote fixedness of thought, singleness of intention, and devotedness of spirit. Whatever is subtle and refined, is in danger of being unscriptural. If we do not guard the mind, it will learn to wander in quest of novelties. It will set more value on original thoughts than devout affections. It is the business of prayer to cast down imaginations which gratify the natural activity of the mind, while they leave the heart unhumbled.

We should confine ourselves to the *present* business of the *present* moment; we should keep the mind in a state of perpetual dependance. "Now is the accepted time." "To-day we must hear his voice." "Give us *this* day our daily bread." The manna will not keep till to-morrow: to-morrow will have its own wants, and must have its own petitions. To-morrow we must seek the bread of heaven afresh.

We should, however, avoid coming to our devotions with unfurnished minds. We should be always laying in materials for prayer, by a diligent course of serious reading, by treasuring up in our minds the most important truths, and by a careful and solemn self-examination. If we rush into the divine presence with a vacant, or ignorant, or unprepared mind, with a heart filled with the world; as we shall feel no disposition or qualification for the work we are about to engage in, so we cannot expect that our petitions will be heard or granted. There must be some congruity between the heart and the object, some affinity between the state of our minds and the business in which they are employed, if we would expect success in the work.

We are often deceived both as to the principle and the effect of our prayers. When from some external cause the heart is glad, the spirits light, the thoughts reasonable, the tongue voluble, a kind of spontaneous eloquence is the result; with this we are pleased, and this ready flow we are ready to impose on ourselves for piety.

On the other hand, when the mind is dejected, the animal spirits low, the thoughts confused; when apposite words do not readily present themselves, we are apt to accuse our hearts of want of fervor, to lament our weakness, and to mourn that, because we have no pleasure in praying, our prayers have, therefore, not ascended to the throne of mercy. In both cases we perhaps judge ourselves unfairly. These unready accents, these faltering praises, these ill-expressed petitions may find more acceptance than the florid talk with which we were so well satisfied: the latter consisted, it may be, of shining thoughts floating on the fancy, eloquent words dwelling only on the lips: the former was the sighing of a contrite heart, abased by the feeling of its own unworthiness, and awed by the perfections of a holy and heart-searching God. The heart is dissatisfied with its own dull and tasteless repetitions, which, with all their imperfections, infinite goodness may perhaps hear with favor. We may not only be elated with the fluency, but even with the fervency of our prayers. Vanity may grow out of the very act of renouncing it, and we may begin to feel proud at having humbled ourselves so eloquently.

There is, however, a strain and spirit of prayer equally distinct from that facility and copiousness for which we certainly are never the better in the sight of God, and from that constraint and dryness for which we may be never the worse. There is a simple, solid, pious strain of prayer, in which the supplicant is so filled and occupied with a sense of his own dependance, and of the importance of the things for which he asks, and so persuaded of the power and grace of God through Christ to give him those things, that while he is engaged in it, he does not merely imagine, but feels assured that God is nigh to him as a reconciled Father, so that every burden and doubt are taken off from his mind. "He knows," as St. John expresses it, "that he has the petition he desired of God," and he feels the truth of that promise, "while they speak I will hear." This is the perfection of prayer.

Prayer is the soul's sincere desire,
Unuttered or expressed;
The motion of a hidden fire
That trembles in the breast.

Prayer is the burden of a sigh,
  The falling of a tear;
The upward glancing of an eye,
  When none but God is near.

Prayer is the simplest form of speech,
  The infant lips can try;
Prayer the sublimest strains that reach
  The majesty on high.

Prayer is the Christian's vital breath,
  The Christian's native air,
His watchwords at the gates of death;
  He enters heaven by prayer.

Prayer is the contrite sinner's voice,
  Returning from his ways,
While angels in their songs rejoice,
  And say, "Behold he prays."

The saints in prayer appear as one,
  In word, and deed, and mind,

When with the Father and the Son,
  Their fellowship they find.

Nor prayer is made on earth alone:
  The Holy Spirit pleads;
And Jesus on the eternal throne,
  For sinners intercedes.

O Thou, by whom we come to God;
  The Life, the Truth, the Way;
The path of prayer thyself hast trod
  Lord, teach us how to pray.

JAMES MONTGOMERY.

See this subject discussed at length, in a work entitled "The Spirit of Prayer," by Hannah More.

THOUGHTS

ON

PRIVATE DEVOTION.

CHAP. I.

THE ADVANTAGES OF PRIVATE PRAYER.

INTRODUCTION.

It is the indispensable duty of every Christian to pray in private.

Our Saviour hath enjoined it on all his followers, by precept, by promise, and by his own blessed example; "When thou prayest, enter into thy closet, and when thou hast shut thy door, pray to thy Father which is in secret, and thy Father which seeth in secret shall reward thee openly."

(Matt. vi. 9.) The precept is positive: the promise is certain: in both the singular number is used. Christ here saith to each of his followers, "Enter into *thy* closet." "Pray to *thy* Father." *Thy* Father shall reward *thee.* As obedience to the divine precepts is generally attended with a present blessing, so is it here. For private prayer sweetly inclines and disposes a person to a cheerful performance of every other religious duty and service; and the power of godliness in the soul flourishes or decays as the private duties of the closet are attended to or neglected. This, in conjunction with the precept, promise, and example of the Saviour, furnishes the true Christian with powerful motives for continuing instant in private prayer even unto the end: when his heavenly Father, who seeth in secret, will, in an especial manner, openly reward him.

The Saviour's example of private prayer arrested the attention of all the evangelists. How often do we read of his sending the multitude away, and going up into a mountain apart to pray! (Matt. xiv. 24. Mark vi. 46.) St. Mark mentions his rising up a great while before day for that purpose. And St. Luke records one instance (doubtless it was not the only one) of his going "out into a mountain to pray, and continuing all night in prayer to God." (Luke vi. 12.) For the sake of private prayer, he would forego the pleasure of conversation with his disciples on the most interesting subjects. When his heart was full of heaviness, and his soul exceeding sorrowful, instead of telling the particulars of the sad tale in the ears of his disciples, who loved him, he said unto them, "Sit ye here, while I go and pray yonder." (Matt. xxvi. 36.) There he unbosomed his soul to his Father, offering up "prayers and supplications, with strong crying and tears, unto him who was able to save him from death, and was heard in that he feared." (Heb. v. 7.)

"Night is the time to pray;
Our Saviour oft withdrew
To desert mountains far away,
So will his followers do;
Steal from the throng to haunts untrod,
And hold communion there with God."

JAMES MONTGOMERY.

What an illustrious example. Did He spend *whole nights* in private prayer on a *cold mountain,* for our sakes; and shall we think it too much to spend a portion of the *day* in our *closets,* for the furtherance of our own spiritual and eternal welfare? Oh, that we were daily imitating more that noble pattern which his holy life exhibits, by being much alone with God! What is Christianity but an imitation of all the inimitable perfections of the Saviour? A Christian's whole life should be a visible representation of Christ. The example of patriarchs, prophets, apostles, and saints, as recorded in the Old and New Testaments, plainly show, that, to be "followers of them who through faith and patience inherit the promises," we should be much in private prayer. But, to the spiritually-minded Christian, the example of Christ vastly transcends all others. Those of the best of men are defective. His alone is the perfect pattern. To be an imitator of him in all his moral virtues is the duty and privilege of a Christian. And, of all others, they are the happiest who come the nearest to his bright example.

PRIVATE PRAYER HAS MANY ADVANTAGES.

In secret we may more freely, fully, and safely unbosom our souls to God, than we can do in the presence of many or few.

In public, confessions of sin are made in general terms. In private, we may descend to particulars. "The heart knoweth his own bitterness." (Prov. xiv. 10.) Every Christian has his secret faults, from which he desires to be cleansed. (Ps. xix. 12). He has not the grosser vices of the ungodly to confess. But, becoming daily more acquainted with the spirituality of God's law, and the deep depravity of his own heart, he feels himself continually prone to err, and discovers within him a variety of things of a sinful nature, which he desires heartily and sincerely to confess at a throne of grace. The thought of foolishness—a proud look—a vain imagination—a sinful inclination—a secret murmur—a repining thought—the slightest indication of an unforgiving temper—the remains of unbelief—secret distrust—carnal reasonings—a want of watchfulness—formality in holy duties—the comparative coldness of his affections towards heavenly things—the smallest degree of worldly-mindedness—the risings of envy, vain-glory, or spiritual pride—the want of love towards God or man—a hasty expression or an unguarded word, though perhaps unobserved by others—these, and a variety of similar things, which at times disturb a pious mind, and grieve his heart, will furnish him with abundant matter for confession before God, in whose word it is written, "He that covereth his sins shall not prosper; but whoso confesseth and forsaketh them shall have mercy." (Prov. xxxviii. 13.) As a patient, afflicted with a loathsome disease, speaks not publicly of all the symptoms of his case, but takes a convenient opportunity of mentioning them to his physician—so the Christian will not publish to the world all the corrupt workings of his heart, which he feels and laments; but, availing himself of the fit opportunity private prayer affords, will freely confess them to his heavenly Physician, Christ Jesus, who alone can forgive all his sins, and heal all the spiritual diseases of the soul.

Confession of sin, however, is but one part of a Christian's duty in his closet. While passing through this vale of tears, he has his peculiar trials, his peculiar wants, and his peculiar mercies. Another will scarcely be found whose experience in all points will accord with his own. In all his trials, wants, and mercies, he alone seems to be deeply interested. No one else can so feelingly express what his sufferings under trials are, the urgency of his wants, or the gratitude he feels for mercies he has received. Hence arises the insufficiency of public and family prayer for every purpose, and the necessity of the Christian's retiring to his closet—where, through our great "High Priest, who is touched with the feeling of our infirmities," he may in secret "come boldly to a throne of grace, and obtain mercy, and find grace to help in every time of need." (Heb. iv. 15, 16.)

Private Prayer is a privilege of which a Christian may at all times avail himself.

Ill health, affliction in his family, unfavorable weather, the distance, and a variety of other circumstances, may detain him from the public means of grace; but none of these can prevent his praying in secret. However desirous he may be of enjoying the benefits of a domestic altar, a want of piety in his friends, or a determined opposition to domestic worship in the heads of his family, may deprive him of this means also. But neither friends nor enemies have power to prevent his holding communion with his God in secret. No time is unseasonable for such a purpose—no place unfit for such devotions. There is no corner so dark—no place so secret, but God is there. He never wants an eye to see, an ear to hear the cries and groans, nor a heart to grant the request, of him who sincerely prays to Him in secret. There are no desires so confused—no requests so broken—no effort so feeble, as to escape his notice. The eye that God hath upon his people in secret, is such a special tender eye of love as opens his ear, his heart, and his hand, for their good. "The eyes of the Lord are over the righteous, and his ears are open to their prayers." Should their petitions be feeble and faint, and seem to them scarcely to reach the heavens, he will graciously *bow down* "his ear, and attend to the prayer that goeth not out of feigned lips." He knows the intentions of the heart. He perceives the motions of the soul. He records them all in the book of his remembrance, and will one day openly reward all these secret transactions. Did Christians more fully believe this, and more seriously consider it—they would live more thankfully, labor more cheerfully, suffer more patiently, fight against the world, the flesh, and the devil, more manfully, and lay themselves out for God, his interests, and glory, more freely.

Private Prayer is a scriptural means of obtaining a clearer knowledge of the revealed will of God.

IT has been compared to a golden key unlocking the mysteries of the divine word. "If any man lack wisdom, let him ask of God." (James i. 5.) The knowledge of many choice and blessed truths is but the returns of private prayer. We have a remarkable instance of this in the history of Cornelius. "At the ninth hour (saith he) I prayed in my house, and behold a man stood by me in bright clothing, and said, Cornelius, thy prayer is heard. (Acts x. 30, 31.) Send men to Joppa and call for Simon, whose sirname is Peter, who shall tell thee words, whereby thou and all thy house shall be saved." (Acts xi. 13, 14.)

His prayer was not only heard and accepted, but graciously answered, in the knowledge he obtained of salvation by Jesus Christ. Another instance may be adduced from the book of Daniel. He was a man who studied the sacred Scriptures, (Dan. ix. 2,) and in answer to prayer, obtained a clearer knowledge of their contents. "While I was speaking and *praying,* and confessing my sin, and the sin of my people Israel, and presenting my supplication before the Lord my God. for the holy mountain of my God; yea, *while I was speaking in prayer,* even the man Gabriel, whom I had seen in the vision at the beginning, being caused to fly swiftly, touched me about the time of the evening oblation; and he informed me, and talked with me, and said, O Daniel, I am now come forth *to give thee skill and understanding.* At the beginning of thy supplications the commandment came forth, and I am come to show thee; for thou art greatly beloved: therefore understand the matter and consider the vision." (Dan. ix. 20, 23.) To "understand the matter"—to have clearer views of the revealed will of God, was a great blessing; but, not a greater than that gracious assurance with which the communication of that knowledge was accompanied, namely, that he was in the favor of God, a "man greatly beloved." Happy is he who in sincerity seeks instruction at the fountain-head of all spiritual wisdom! The Holy Ghost is promised *to teach us all things.* (John xiv. 26.) The promises of God should be pleaded in prayer. He loves to be sued on his own bond; and delights to lade the wings of secret prayer with his sweetest, choicest, richest blessings. Hence it is that the word of Christ dwells most richly in them who are most diligent and fervent in pouring out their hearts to him in secret.

Those who piously and conscientiously discharge the duties of the closet generally prosper both in temporals and spirituals.

"GODLINESS is profitable unto all things, having promise of the life that now is and of that which is to come." (1 Tim. iv. 8.) To enter on the duties of our calling in the fear of God, and to do all with a view to his glory, is the surest way to obtain the blessing of Heaven. Temporal affairs are best expedited when they are made the subjects of secret prayer. Generally speaking, he who prays fervently in his closet, will speed well in his shop, at the plough, or in whatsoever he may turn his hand unto. "Them that honor me (saith the Lord), I will honor; and they that despise me shall be lightly esteemed." (1 Sam. ii. 30.) All the worthies, who are mentioned in Scripture as men of private prayer, prospered in the world. God blessed to them their blessings, and eventually made their cup of temporal mercies to overflow. And in the last great day, when God shall judge the secrets of men by Jesus Christ, and shall openly reward them that have prayed to him secretly, it will be manifest to assembled worlds, that no families have been so prospered, protected and blessed, as those who have been most diligent in maintaining secret communion with Him.

As to spiritual things, it is most certain that private devotion prepares the heart, and fits the soul, so to speak, for the public duties of religion. He who willingly neglects one has seldom much enjoyment in the other. But he who in secret waits upon God sincerely, will, in the public means, frequently find his spiritual strength renewed, his languishing graces revived, his intercourse with Heaven more pure, his hopes more elevated, and his enjoyments more spiritual. Want of private prayer may be one great reason why many are so heavy and dull, so formal and careless, so unfruitful and lifeless, under the public means of grace. Oh, that Christians would seriously lay this to heart! He who would have his soul athirst for God, and long to see his goings in the sanctuary, (Psalm lxiii. 1, 2,) who would have public ordinances lovely and delightful to his soul, his drooping spirits refreshed, his weak faith strengthened, his strong corruptions subdued, and his affections set on heavenly things (Col. iii. 2), should be frequent and fervent in secret prayer. How strong in grace—how victorious over sin—how dead to the world—how alive to Christ—how fit to live—how prepared to die—might many a Christian have been, had he more diligently, seriously, and conscientiously discharged the duties of the closet!

Diligence and perseverance in secret prayer may be regarded as a certain evidence of sincerity.

Private prayer is not the hypocrite's delight. He can find no solid satisfaction in such exercises. He loves to pray where others may notice his devotions and commend him; and he has his reward. (Matt. vi. 5.) The Scriptures record nothing of Saul and Judas, Demas and Simon Magus, that affords the slightest evidence of their having addicted themselves to secret prayer. The Scribes and Pharisees assumed the garb of exterior sanctity, but we never read of their retiring to a solitary place to pray. A good name among men is more valued by a hypocrite than a good life or a good conscience. Under some temporary alarm he may cry aloud upon his bed, or seek relief on his knees in retirement. But, "Will he delight himself in the Almighty? will he *always* call upon God?" (Job xxvii. 10.) If the cause be removed, the effect will cease. When his fears have subsided, and his spirits are tranquillized, he will discontinue the practice, laying aside his private prayers as an irksome task. Secret duties are not his ordinary work. Self is the oil of his lamp;—worldly interests and the plaudits of men nourish its flame. If these are wanting, its brilliancy declines; and, as his hope of these fail, its light gradually or instantly expires. "Can the rush grow up without mire?—can the flag grow without water?—whilst it is yet in its greenness, and not cut down, it withereth before any other herb. So are the paths of all that forget God: and the hypocrite's hope shall perish." (Job viii. 11, 13.)

He does not "*forget God*, who perseveres in the duties of the closet." God is the object, and his glory the end, of his secret devotions. He retires from the observation of men to "give unto the Lord the glory due unto his name, (and to) worship the Lord in the beauty of holiness." (Ps. xxix. 2.) He is not satisfied with a mere external performance of the duty. He examines his motives, scrutinizes the workings of his heart, and afterwards reviews the whole transaction. "I call to remembrance my song in the night: I commune with my own heart: my spirit made diligent search." (Ps. lxxvii. 6.) Not so the hypocrite. "Praying *always*, with *all* prayer and supplication in the spirit, and *watching thereunto* with all *perseverance*," (Eph. vi. 18,) is not his practice. He has ever at hand some excuse for the neglect of *private* prayer. Though he squanders perhaps every day more than an hour of his time in frivolous conversation or unnecessary visitings, he can persuade himself his engagements are so many and so urgent, that he has no time for retiring to his closet without neglecting his worldly business, in which he must be diligent from a regard to the divine precept (Rom xii. 11,) and for his family's sake. Or, should his conscience testify that he has time sufficient, another circumstance will furnish him with an excuse—the want of a convenient place. Oh, let it ever be remembered, that the most illustrious example we have of diligence and perseverance in this sacred duty, namely, Christ Jesus, was pressed for time more than any man, through a multiplicity of other engagements; so much so, that at times he "had no leisure so much as to eat." (Mark vi. 31.) And as to place, "The foxes have holes, and the birds of the air have nests, but the Son of Man (had) not where to lay his head." (Matt. viii. 20.) Yet, by rising early, and by late retiring to rest, (compare Mark i. 35, with Luke vi. 12,) he found sufficient time; and in the open air, on a mountain, or in a garden, a convenient place for pouring out his soul to God. The hypocrite wants a *heart* for it, more than he wants sufficient time or a convenient place. However regular he may be in his attendance on public prayer, he does not *love private,* and, therefore, does not habituate himself to the practice of it. He it is who *loves* to pray secretly, and values such exercises for the effect they have on him in humbling the soul, mortifying pride, debasing self, weaning the heart from the world, imbittering sin, rendering the mind more spiritual, and exalting the Saviour in the affections; who habituates himself to, and perseveres in the practice of, secret prayer. And a diligent and conscientious continuing in such well-doing, most assuredly affords a decisive evidence of sincerity.

There is no means of grace more enriching to the soul than private prayer.

It is a golden pipe, through which the Lord is graciously pleased to convey spiritual blessings to the soul. He knoweth all our wants, and, without our asking him, could supply all our need in the best manner, and at the best possible time. But he will be inquired of by the house of Israel, to do for them according to the exceeding great and precious promises he hath given. (Ezek. xxxvi. 37.) How often has the believer found the Lord's promises of grace *here* verified, and been enabled to look forward, with joyful hope, to the fulfilment of those which relate to glory hereafter, while he has been engaged in his private devotions! When he has entered his closet, he has been, perhaps, like the mother of Samuel, "*of a sorrowful spirit,*" and, like her, has poured out his "*soul before the Lord,*" with an "*abundance of complaint and grief;*" but *the God of Israel has granted his petition,* and he hath gone on his way with a "countenance no longer sad." (1 Sam. i. 15, 18.) How often in these private exercises, particularly when the believer has felt himself "in heaviness through manifold temptations," (1 Pet. i. 6,) "encompassed with infirmities," (Heb. v. 2,) and has "groaned being burdened," (2 Cor. v. 4,) not knowing "what he should pray for as he ought," (Rom. viii. 26,) hath the Holy Spirit helped his infirmities!—"making him to know his transgression and his sin," (Job. xiii. 23,) and causing him to "abhor himself and repent as in dust and ashes." (Job xliii. 6.) Then, in the language of the Psalmist, he hath prayed:—"The troubles of my heart are enlarged; Oh, bring thou me out of my distresses! (Ps. xxv. 17.) "I will bless the Lord, who hath given me counsel; my reins also chasten me." (Ps. xvi. 7.) "Make me to hear joy and gladness, that the bones which thou hast broken may rejoice. Hide thy face from my sins, and blot out all mine iniquities. Create in me a clean heart, O God, and renew a right spirit within me. Cast me not away from thy presence, and take not thy Holy Spirit from me. Restore unto me the joy of thy salvation: and uphold me with thy free Spirit." (Ps. li. 8, 12.) God hath heard this prayer, and fulfilled his own most gracious word:—"Before they call I will answer, and while they are yet speaking, I will hear." (Isa. lxv. 24.) The Saviour's promise also hath been verified:—"He that hath my commandments, and keepeth them, he it is that loveth me: and he that loveth me shall be loved of my Father, and I will love him, and will manifest myself to him." (John xiv. 21.) The Holy Spirit hath taken of the things of Jesus, and hath shown them unto his servant, (John xvi. 14,) and the believer hath been enabled with lively gratitude and joy, to adopt the language of the prophet. "O Lord, I will praise thee: though thou wast angry with me, thine anger is turned away, and thou comfortest me. Behold, God is my salvation; I will trust, and not be afraid: for the Lord Jehovah is my strength and my song; he is also become my salvation. Therefore with joy shall (I) draw water out of the wells of salvation." (Isa. xii. 1–3.) Thus the Christian, withdrawn for a season from the world, and realising the immediate presence of God, the awfulness of eternity, and the vast importance of heavenly things, prays to his Father, which seeth in secret; gets more humbling views of himself, and makes fresh discoveries of the exceeding sinfulness of sin, and of the superaboundings of Divine grace, of the long-suffering patience of the Lord, of the grace he has bestowed on him, the deliverances he has wrought for him, and the abundant mercy which is treasured up in Christ Jesus for all true believers. Thus he, who began his secret prayers "with groanings that cannot be uttered," (Rom. viii. 26,) finds spiritual enlargement; is "strengthened with might in the inner man," (Eph. iii. 16;) is enriched with the light of God's reconciled countenance; and comes forth from his closet in a more humble, more watchful, more spiritual, more holy, more heavenly frame; and, consequently, is more fit for the public duties of religion, or the particular duties of his calling—the Lord having put into his heart more gladness than an increase of corn and wine could give, (Ps. iv. 7,) and caused his holy comforts to delight his soul. (Psalm xciv. 19.)

CHAP. II.

ON THE NEGLECT OF PRIVATE PRAYER.

How lamentable is it that a duty so obvious, a privilege so great, a means of grace so enriching to the soul, ever should be neglected! What are the causes to be assigned for it?

If the neglect be total and permanent, impenitency of heart may be suspected as the cause.

To perceive no necessity for secret prayer—to have no mind, no will, no heart to such a duty—to make no effort to discharge it, and to feel no remorse of conscience for neglecting it, are fearful signs of an unhumbled, unrenewed, impenitent heart. Whilst the cause remains, the effect will continue; therefore, let such "*beseech God to grant them true repentance and his Holy Spirit,*" that their indisposition to call upon him in private may be removed, that their secret prayers may be accepted, and openly rewarded, by him, "*and that the rest of their life may be pure and holy, so that at the last they may come to his eternal joy, through Jesus Christ our Lord.*"

If the neglect be temporary and voluntary, some sin or sins committed against light and knowledge may be the cause.

Such sins load the conscience with guilt, weaken the spiritual strength of the Christian, becloud his evidences of grace, make him a terror to himself, and afraid of realizing the Divine Presence. Then he is shy of drawing near to God in secret; and as our first parents, from conscious guilt, would have "hid themselves from the presence of the Lord God, amongst the trees of the garden;" so he, by neglecting the positive and known duty of secret prayer, flies, as it were, from the Lord's presence, to forget his transgression and acquire his former confidence, by occupying his time and thoughts with the affairs of this world. But this is folly. To add sin to sin—the sin of omission to the sin of commission—gives the enemy of souls a powerful advantage over him. It invariably increases his guilt, benumbs his conscience, strengthens his inbred corruptions, and renders his return to spiritual duties increasingly difficult. However painful it may be to draw near to God in secret, with an awful consciousness of guilt on the soul, it should not be shunned. It is vastly better, while the conscience is feelingly alive to the wound it has received, to hasten to the throne of grace, and ingeniously to confess the sin, looking to the cross of Christ, and imploring the pardon of it for his sake, and grace to be more watchful in future. It must be done, or the consequences will be most awful; and the sooner it is done the better, "For with the Lord there is mercy, and with him is plenteous redemption, and he shall redeem Israel from all his iniquities." (Ps. cxxx. 7, 8.)

If the neglect be partial, spiritual declension is probably the cause.

WHILE the believer, with deep humiliation, reviews the evils of his past life—reflects upon the awful consequences of sin, and contemplates, with adoring gratitude, the astonishing love of God his Father, the amazing condescension of God the Son, and the stupendous work of God my of redemption, and feels "the love of God shed abroad in his heart," (Rom. v. 5,) he does not neglect the private duties of the closet; but anticipates with delight the return of those seasons of private prayer in which he has frequently enjoyed sweet communion with the Lord, and found his service perfect freedom.

Having "escaped the pollutions of the world," and being watchful lest he be "again entangled therein and overcome," (2 Pet. ii. 20,) a temptation from that quarter excites his alarm, leads him to his closet, and makes him more earnest in prayer; thus the purposes of the enemy in presenting the temptation are defeated. But he is liable to an attack in a more vulnerable part. Religion is his delight. An evil in a religious garb he does not suspect.

Ignorant in some measure of the devices of his spiritual adversary, he has little or no apprehension of meeting him transformed into an angel of light. He is not aware of the paralyzing effects which an inordinate zeal for the non-essentials of religion has upon the inner man ; nor of the intoxicating nature of that busy, prying curiosity which intrudes *too far* into those mysterious and deep things of God and religion, which are most remote from the understanding of the best and wisest of men. Having tasted much of the pleasantness of religion, and being anxious in the pursuit of more, he eagerly grasps at anything that may be urged by those whom he highly esteems and regards as fathers in Christ, as absolutely necessary to render his Christianity more pure and primitive, or to increase his measure of religious knowledge. This is an important crisis—a time of much spiritual danger: the enemy of souls is ever watchful to hinder the Christian in his course: whatever diverts his attention from the weightier matters of religion to those which are comparatively unimportant, does this. Hence it is, that such as have their thoughts more occupied with the non-essentials of religion than with the power of godliness in the soul, seldom make much progress in humility or heavenly-mindedness, and are often lamentably deficient in the duties of the closet.

The temptations of the enemy which have the semblance of religion are the most artful. What is called a religious controversy—a dispute about the government and discipline of Christian churches —the modes of public worship and administering the ordinances of baptism and the Lord's supper—or on some abstruse theological subject, often succeeds. Perplexed with the discordant opinions of the controversionists, the pious Christian laudably resolves to examine and weigh for himself the arguments on both sides; on the issue of his inquiry much depends. If, happily, he discovers that the disputation does not relate to matters affecting religion itself, but to non-essentials, concerning which good men may decidedly differ, without the smallest diminution of liberality, or Christian forbearance, towards those of a contrary opinion; it is well. His perplexity ceases, and his heart is enlarged in Christian love towards all who love the Lord Jesus Christ in sincerity; and he finds additional pleasure in his secret prayers, when, in giving vent to the pious feelings of his soul, he copiously intercedes for the universal Church of Christ. But if, unhappily, he conceives the disputable articles to be very important, and imbibes a controversial spirit, he receives a wound materially affecting his spiritual health—his mental appetite becomes vitiated—he cannot feed on the most important truths unless the mode of serving them up precisely fit his humour. His zeal is soon diverted to a new channel, and his thoughts are wholly occupied with arguments in support of his favorite position. He begins to feed, as it were, on the very husks of religion.

A vast declension in spiritual things takes place in him, and he perceives it not. He frequently neglects private prayer: (not voluntarily indeed, but) having his mind fully occupied with things that have the semblance of religion, he *forgets* to retire; when he recollects himself, he hastens to his closet; should the work of his favorite author in the controversy be near his Bible, he cannot resist the temptation to read just a page or two in that. He reads: he finds his time almost gone; the reading of the Scriptures is postponed to a more convenient opportunity, that he may spend his few remaining moments in prayer. With his lips he goes over, as it were, mechanically, a few important petitions, whilst a multitude of thoughts are rushing into his mind. *This* corroborates his own arguments; *that* refutes the argument of an opponent. He rises from his knees with a mind, as he conceives, stored with wisdom: he feels himself qualified, had he the power to reorganize the Church, to introduce such a mode of worship and discipline, and so to define the most abstruse points of doctrine, as would, unquestionably, meet the views and wishes of all, and effectually put his opponents to the blush. But where is that humility, that Christian love, that hatred of sin, that watchfulness against pride, self-conceit, and vain-glory, which the Christian ought ever to seek diligently and earnestly in private prayer? Alas, the crown is fallen from his head!

Non-essentials have no place in heaven;

doubtful disputations never enter there; controversial knowledge is no qualification or meetness for the saints in light. Happy is he who avoids disputes about things indifferent, and learns to admire, in the Scriptures, the depths he cannot reach, and to adore the mysteries he cannot comprehend.

If the Christian conceive in his heart an excessive desire of some temporal good, how lawful soever the possession of the thing may be in itself, the effect will be very similar: spiritual declension will succeed, and private prayer will be neglected; though less in the form, probably, than in the spirit of it.

An inordinate desire of any thing, not inseparably connected with religion, engrosses the attention, and pre-occupies the thoughts to the exclusion of meditation, the handmaid of private devotion; and like "the cares of this world" in general, and "the deceitfulness of riches" in particular, chokes the precious seed, and renders it unfruitful. With his affections thus embarrassed, the Christian may retire to his closet, but the object which he is pursuing with impassionate ardour will follow him thither. He may bend his knees, but the ardently desired good will present itself, in its most engaging forms, to his imagination, and possess his thoughts. He may draw nigh unto God with his lips, "but his heart will be far from him;" for "where his treasure is, there will his heart be also."

Should an apparently favorable opportunity present itself for pursuing the object of his inordinate desire, at the very period of time he has been accustomed to retire for private prayer, a barter of time succeeds. His prayers are deferred to another opportunity, and the present fortunate moment, as he conceives, eagerly seized as most fit for prosecuting his favorite schemes. But no time is found for his secret devotions, till the accustomed period again returns. Thus in the form, as well as the spirit of it, is secret prayer neglected, through an inordinate desire of some temporal good. *He who has left his first love should remember from whence he hath fallen, and repent, and do his first works.* (Rev. ii. 4, 5.)

Whatever be the cause, the neglect of secret prayer is culpable and dangerous.

It gives the enemy an advantage against the soul, and, by damping the ardor of spiritual affections, strengthens inbred corruptions. It fosters spiritual sloth, engenders earthly mindedness, blunts the edge of conscience, induces a laxity of Christian morals, and eventually, if persevered in, an indisposition to the public duties of religion. It should be dreaded as an alarming indication of indifference to the promised help of the Holy Spirit, and an awful slighting of the rich mercies tendered to us in the Gospel. How very different is every instance of real neglect, in its character and consequences, to that imaginary kind over which the pious Christian sometimes mourns. Incapacitated for retiring to his closet, by some bodily disease, which renders the constant attendance of another person upon him necessary, he is deprived of the opportunities of private devotion, for which he thirsts, and is frequently interrupted when mentally calling on his God. Being thus prevented from pouring out his heart before the Lord, with all that copiousness and enlargement he could desire (though he prays sincerely and very earnestly in the way of ejaculation,) he feels a deficiency; and, without considering the circumstances under which he is placed, suspects himself of neglect, and is much grieved. This is his infirmity; it is not neglect, though it seems to him to be such. If the cause were removed, the effect would immediately cease. He does not *voluntarily* absent himself from his closet; his heart is still *there;* and thither would he resort, if restored to health. In the meantime, the secret aspirations of his soul will be favorably regarded, and will ultimately be openly rewarded by his heavenly Father, as prayers offered to him in secret.

In like manner the Christian may suspect himself guilty of some neglect of secret prayer, when his mind is affected, and his animal spirits are depressed with some corporal malady which does not confine him to his apartments, but unfits his mind for exertion, and disqualifies him for bending his knees in prayer, or prevents his continuing long in that position. Under such an affliction he may feel (if kneeling) much lassitude, his thoughts confused, his desires languid, his affections cold, his petitions faint, his praises inanimate, and be much grieved; ascribing to it an indisposition to private prayer, bordering on a neglect of the duty; because, in another position of body, he feels himself very differently affected with spiritual things. But, can this be neglect? Does it border upon it? He has a mind, a will, a heart, to pray in secret; and, notwithstanding his bodily indisposition, makes an effort to do so.—"The spirit is willing, but the flesh is weak." The lamented deficiencies of his prayers will be graciously pardoned, and his imperfect petitions mercifully accepted and answered; for his heavenly Father, who seeth in secret, "searcheth the heart, and knoweth what is the mind of the spirit" (Rom. viii. 27;) and will register the sorrowful sighings of his contrite ones, to be openly rewarded, in the last Great Day.

It will, doubtless, be evident to those who are disposed to practice it—that secret prayer is the duty of all; that its advantages are many and great; and that the neglect of it is sinful and dangerous. For the benefit of such shall be added a few directions for a devout discharge of so important and necessary a duty.

CHAP. III.

A FEW DIRECTIONS FOR A DEVOUT DISCHARGE OF THIS IMPORTANT AND NECESSARY DUTY.

Private Prayer, as a means, tends to counteract the corrupt workings of the heart, and to give a proper bias to the faculties of the soul; it should therefore be performed frequently.

It is far better to pray *often*, than to make *long prayers*. As in our taking frequently a temperate supply of fresh nourishment, the Lord *providentially* repairs the continual wastes of our bodies, and keeps the fluids in a healthy state; so, in our frequent use of private prayer, he *graciously* restores the soul (Ps. xxiii. 3,) and causes it to prosper and be in health. (3 John 2.) The Christian, therefore, cannot too frequently contemplate and desire heavenly treasures. He cannot too frequently approach his blessed Saviour, and hold communion with his God in secret prayer.

The fittest season should be taken for this sacred duty.

Some, who are subject to drowsiness in the after part of the day, prefer the morning before their minds have been occupied, and their spirits damped, with temporal concerns. And it is doubtless most fit that God should be worshipped by every one, before he enters on the business of the day. Others, who are constitutionally heavy and dull in the morning, and almost unfit for any thing, are quite alert in the evening, and exempt from that heaviness, of which so many complain, as peculiarly unfitting them for prayer. Every one, therefore, must be left to determine, which, in his case are the fittest parts of the day to be the stated period of his private devotions. But the Christian's experience varies. There are seasons when he feels his mind more than usually solemnized, and every thing connected with religion appears to him of the utmost importance. His conscience at one time is peculiarly tender, his soul within him deeply humbled under a sense of sin, his heart broken and contrite, and he is very sorrowful. At another, his faith in the promise of God is vigorous, his hope animated, his love to the Saviour ardent, and he is very thankful. Seasons like these should be embraced, as especially fit to be extraordinary times of secret devotion.

The Christian should be constant in the discharge of his duty.

It is not very probable that the incalculable benefits of it should be experimentally known by those who retire to their closets by fits and starts only. If it be necessary for a man to pray in secret when he is suffering from the upbraidings of his conscience, or smarting under the rod of affliction; it is equally so in the time of prosperity, when it is probable his danger is greater, and fresh trials may await him. The Christian should "pray without ceasing." Not actually, indeed; for private prayer, like every other kind, must have its intermissions; but the heart should be in a disposition for it, at all times, in all places, and under all circumstances, and in the actual practice of it, at fit times, he should persevere. It is not he who begins in the spirit and ends in the flesh, but he that endureth to the end, that will be saved.

Important as secret prayer is, and necessary to his soul's health, it must not be trusted in.

CHRIST alone is the foundation of our hope. If we are not interested in him, we may perish with the words of prayer on our lips. (Matt. xxv. 11, 12.) It is the Saviour's free grace, infinite mercy, everlasting love—his full, perfect, and sufficient sacrifice, oblation, and satisfaction—his pure, spotless, perfect, and glorious righteousness, which form the proper basis of the Christian's trust and confidence. He must not, therefore, trust in his prayers, but in his Saviour; and doubtless the enemy of his soul will tremble to see him go, and leave his closet, trusting and glorying alone in Jesus. Thrice happy is he, whose secret prayers lead him, as the star led the eastern Magii, to the feet of the Saviour!—and who, like them, when there, is disposed willingly to offer the choicest and best things he has, not indeed "gold and frankincense and myrrh," but himself, his soul and body, to be a reasonable, holy, and lively sacrifice unto God.

The Christian, in all his prayers, should look well to his heart.

The eye of God is then, in an especial manner, upon it. He does not look at the eloquence, the length, the number of the prayers, but at the sincerity of the heart.

He approves, accepts and rewards no prayer, but that in which the heart is engaged. It is not the lifting up of the voice, the wringing of the hands, or the smiting on the breast, that he regards, but the motions of the heart. He hears with approbation no more than the heart speaks in sincerity.

Every prayer should be offered in the name of Jesus.

THROUGH him alone we have access with boldness to the throne of grace. He is our advocate with the Father. When the believer appears before God in secret, the Saviour appears also: for he "ever liveth to make intercession for us." He hath not only directed us to call upon his Father as "Our Father," and to ask him to supply our daily need, and to forgive us our trespasses; but hath graciously assured us that "*whatsoever* (we) shall ask *in his name,* he will do it, that the Father may be glorified in the Son." (John, xiv. 13.) And saith (14th verse,) "if ye shall ask *anything in my name,* I will do it." And again (John xvi. 23, 24.) "Verily, verily, I say unto you, whatsoever ye shall ask the Father *in my name* he will give it you. Hitherto have ye asked nothing *in my name;* ask, and *ye shall receive,* that your joy may be full." All needful blessings suited to our various situations and circumstances in this mortal life,—all that will be necessary for us in the hour of death, and all that can minister to our felicity in a world of glory, hath he graciously promised, and given us a command to ask for, *in his name.* And what is this but to plead, when praying to our heavenly Father, that Jesus hath sent us; and to ask and expect the blessings for his sake alone?

Expect therefore an answer to prayer.

"I WILL make an altar (said the venerable patriarch Jacob) unto God, who answereth me in the day of my distress, and was with me in the way which I went." (Gen. xxxv. 3.) He expected the blessing which he asked of the Lord, and in the dispensations of Providence towards him he received the answer to his prayer.

God is faithful, who hath promised. He

saith, concerning every one who "hath set his love upon" him, "He shall *call upon me* and I will *answer him,* I will be with him in trouble; I will deliver him and honor him." (Ps. xci. 14, 15.) His promises are evidently designed to direct us in our supplications, and to excite in us an expectation of their fulfilment. And what is prayer but the offering up of the desires of the heart for some good thing, which the Lord hath directly or indirectly promised in his holy word to bestow? The very act itself implies that a blessing may be vouchsafed, in answer to our petitions; and his promises assure us there will; though the time and manner of conferring it are reserved to himself: and he best knows what will suit us, and the best possible time of bestowing it. Therefore, he who obeys the divine precepts heartily, pleads the promises in prayer perseveringly, waits their fulfilment patiently, and is content if God be glorified, though himself be not gratified, may confidently expect seasonable and suitable answers to all the prayers he offers in sincerity at a throne of grace, in the name of Jesus.

PRIVATE DEVOTION.

PART II.

MORNING AND EVENING PRAYERS, FOR EVERY DAY IN THE WEEK, AND ON VARIOUS OCCASIONS; DEVOUT MEDITATIONS; A COURSE OF SELF-EXAMINATION; AND DEVOTIONAL POETRY.

"It cannot be supposed that persons who use the following forms of prayer are under the necessity of confining themselves to every expression and sentiment in them. Any words or sentences may be added, omitted, or changed, as they see occasion, to suit their present state, their own judgment of things, and their circumstances. For it can never be expected that the same method or form of private prayer should suit all persons at all times. It is impossible that a serious Christian can present to God in secret prayer all his wants, all his sorrows, all his dearest and most important concerns, in a few general sentences pre-composed by another."

AN INTRODUCTORY

MEDITATION ON PRAYER.

BY BISHOP WILSON.

How good is God! who will not only give us what we pray for, but will reward us for going to him, and laying our wants before him.

May I always present myself before God, with a firm faith and hope in his promises and mercy;—with great reverence to his infinite majesty;—with the humility of an offender;—and with a full purpose of keeping of God's commandments.

May the thoughts of eternity quicken my devotions;—my wants make me earnest; my backslidings make me persevere; —and may I never wilfully give way to any distracting thoughts.

May I wait with patience, and leave it to thee, my God and Father, *how* and *when* to grant my petitions.

He that has learned to pray as he ought, has got the *secret* of a holy life.

It is of greater advantage to us than we imagine, that God does not grant our petitions immediately. We learn by *that*, that whereunto we have already attained, *it was the gift of God.*

The best way to prevent wandering in prayer is not to let the mind wander too much at other times: but to have God always in our minds in the whole course of our lives. The end of prayer is not to inform God, but to give a man a sight of his own misery; to raise his soul towards heaven; and to put him in mind that there is his Father and his inheritance.

MORNING PRAYERS.

SUNDAY.

O LORD, I desire to begin the day and the week with thee. Let a solemn sense of thy presence be upon my mind; and while I offer my supplications, in the name of my only Mediator, the Lord Jesus Christ, comfort my heart by the assurance that thou art nigh unto all them that call upon thee, even all such as call upon thee faithfully.

I acknowledge before thee, O Lord, how unworthy I am to be numbered with thy children, for I have sinned against thee, and thy wrath might justly have consumed me in a moment, and have sent me down to hell:—but thou hast had mercy on me, and hast made known unto me by thy word how I may be saved.

I thank thee, O Lord, for the opportunities which I am invited to enjoy this day, of hearing those blessed truths, the knowledge of which is essential to the salvation of my soul. Oh! give me grace diligently to attend to thy word, enable me to understand it, and make me anxious to improve by it; that the sermons which I hear may not rise up against me at the great day.

Bless, O gracious God, the ministers of thy Gospel, especially my own, who show unto us the way of salvation. Do thou teach them, that they may be able to teach us. O Lord, may thy word this day awaken my conscience, that I may see more evil in the nature of sin, more danger from the guilt of it, and be more earnest to secure an interest in Christ, the only Saviour.

I beseech thee, O Lord, to keep me this day from all worldly thoughts and words; and may thy Spirit suggest such things to my mind as are suitable to this holy part of my time. Oh, may I keep thy Sabbath in a becoming manner, and love it as the best day of the seven, because it is a season dedicated to thy service! Preserve me, whilst in thy house, from a stupid and a wandering frame; strengthen my memory to retain what I hear, and make this day a time of real benefit to my soul, for which I may have reason to bless thee to all eternity, for Jesus Christ's sake. Amen.

Our Father, &c.

MONDAY.

Almighty and most merciful Father! thou art a God that hearest prayer; and I am encouraged to draw nigh unto thy throne of grace, most humbly beseeching thee to look upon me according to thy tender mercy in Jesus Christ. I confess my daily offences against thee, in thought, word, and deed. If thou shouldst be extreme to mark what is done amiss, O Lord, who might abide it! Deal not with me after my sins, neither reward me after my iniquities. I bless thee for that all-pervading advocate, Jesus Christ, the righteous: by his cross and intercession, good Lord, deliver me.

I am now about to enter upon the

worldly employments of another week: strengthen me with thy grace, that these may not withdraw my heart from thee, nor make me negligent of my soul, and my salvation. May the influences of the Sabbath rest upon me through the week; and may the solemn and blessed truths which I heard yesterday, in the house of prayer, abide in my memory and direct my conduct!

With many thanks for thy mercies during the past night, I now cast myself upon thy protection, not knowing what this day may bring forth; but trusting in that wisdom which cannot err, and in that love which cannot fail; do thou appoint my lot as seemeth good to both. Father, not my will, but thine be done! Preserve me from temptation; preserve me from sin; preserve me from my own evil heart; and if I am permitted to see the close of this day, let me look back upon it, as one in which I have walked with God; through Jesus Christ, my Redeemer and Advocate. Amen.

Our Father, &c.

TUESDAY.

[Dr. Johnson.

O God, who desireth not the death of a sinner, look down with mercy on me, now daring to call upon thee. Let thy Holy Spirit so purify my affections and exalt my desires, that my prayers may be acceptable in thy sight, through Jesus Christ.

O merciful God, full of compassion, long suffering, and of great pity, who sparest when we deserve punishment, and in thy wrath thinkest upon mercy, make me earnestly to repent and be heartily sorry for all my misdoings; make the remembrance of them so burthensome and painful, that I may flee unto thee with a troubled spirit and a contrite heart; and, O merciful Lord, visit, comfort, and relieve me; cast me not out of thy presence, and take not thy Holy Spirit from me, but excite in me true repentance; give me in this world knowledge of thy truth, and confidence in thy mercy, and in the world to come life everlasting. Forgive the days and years which I have passed in folly, idleness, and sin; fill me with such sorrow for the time mis-spent, that I may amend my life according to thy holy word; strengthen me against sin, and enable me so to perform every duty, that whilst I live I may serve thee in that state to which thou hast called me, and at last, by a holy and happy death, be delivered from the struggles and sorrows of this life, and obtain eternal happiness, by the mercy and for the sake of Jesus Christ. Amen.

Our Father, &c.

WEDNESDAY.

[Bp. Bloomfield.

O God, thou art my God; early will I seek thee. Thou art good, and doest good to all; thy mercy is over all thy works.

Unworthy as I am to offer unto thee any sacrifice, thou hast appointed unto me a great High Priest, in whose name I come boldly to the throne of grace, that I may find mercy and grace to help me in time of need.

Grant that the frequency and earnestness of my prayers may be proportioned to the greatness of my wants. Make me to rejoice in every opportunity of worshipping thy divine Majesty, and preserve me from the sin of drawing near to thee with my lips, while my heart is far from thee.

I humbly thank thee, O Lord, that thou hast preserved me through the night past, and hast renewed unto me thy goodness this morning. Take me again into thy guidance and protection during the day; and so govern me by thy grace, that I may neither think nor speak, nor do anything this day which may displease thee or wound my own soul. Assist me to be sincere and hearty in dedicating myself, my soul and body, to thy service. Preserve me from the power of evil; from the sin that doth so easily beset me; from the lusts of the flesh, and the vanities of a wicked world.

Send thy good spirit to direct and guide me in the ways and works of godliness: purify my affections; enliven my devotion; teach me how to pray, and how to hear, and read, and profit by thy holy word. Make me a Christian, not only in name, but also in heart and hope. Teach me the value of my soul and the salvation which has been wrought for it by Christ Jesus. May I never be ashamed of confessing him before men; but amidst all discouragements and difficulties, give me boldness to show myself his true disciple.

Let my conversation be such as becometh his Gospel; and whatsoever I do in word or in deed, let me do all in his name, giving thanks to God and the Father through him. And let the words of my mouth, and the meditation of my heart be acceptable in thy sight, O Lord my strength, and my Redeemer. Amen.

Our Father, &c.

THURSDAY.

[Hannah More.

O Lord God Almighty, I thank thee for having preserved me through the past night, and for granting me health and strength for my duties on this day. Blessed be the Lord for all his mercies; for giving me food to eat and raiment to put on, and for delivering me from many evils which my sins have justly deserved.

I thank thee especially, O Lord, for the gift of Jesus Christ thy Son. I confess before thee my exceeding guilt, and I pray thee, for Christ's sake, to pardon my offences, and to receive my soul when I die

I beseech thee also, for his sake, to grant unto me the help of thy Holy Spirit, that I may be enabled to follow my Saviour's example, and to do whatsoever he hath commanded. May I be patient, humble, kind, and merciful; endeavoring to do good unto all men, and forgiving those who trespass against me, even as I hope to be forgiven. Grant me grace this day diligently to perform its duties, and to be true and just in all my dealings, doing unto others as I would they should do unto me; and help me, O Lord, to restrain my tongue, and to subdue my evil tempers, and to live in temperance, soberness, and chastity. Save me from those sins which in times past have most easily beset me; strengthen me, O Lord, for all that awaits me; carry me through all my difficulties and troubles, and help me, day by day, to grow in grace, and in the knowledge of my Lord and Saviour. These prayers I humbly offer up in the name of Jesus Christ. Amen.

Our Father, &c.

FRIDAY.

Almighty and adorable God, permitted by thy kindness to come again into thy presence, I would begin the day with praise to thee who hast given me a night of mercy. Bless the Lord, O my soul: and all that is within me, bless his holy name!

I would sanctify all the employments, and all the events of this day, by placing myself and them in thy care, humbly and earnestly beseeching thee to overrule all things concerning me to thy glory, and the good of my soul. Unto thee do I lift up mine eyes, O thou that dwellest in the heavens! O take me into thy protection, bodily and spiritually. I am ignorant, let thy Spirit teach me; I am guilty, let me obtain pardon through the blood of thy Son; I am a wandering sheep, let thy love lead me to the Saviour's fold; I am in danger from enemies who lie in wait for my soul; what then is my hope? Truly my hope is even in thee. Hold up my goings in thy paths, that my footsteps slip not; keep me as the apple of thine eye; hide me under the shadow of thy wings.

I am in the midst of an ensnaring world; O thou God of all grace, preserve me from the lust of the flesh, the lust of the eyes, and the pride of life! Teach me that the world passeth away, and the lust thereof; while only they who do thy will abide forever. Let me place thee, O my unerring director, always before me: be thou at my right hand continually, lest I make shipwreck of faith and of a good conscience. Leave me not, neither forsake me, O God of my salvation! for thy dear Son Jesus Christ's sake.—Amen.

Our Father, &c,

SATURDAY.

[Bp. Bloomfield.

Almighty and most merciful Father, who, for my many sins committed against thee mightest most justly have cut me off in the midst of my days, I humbly thank thee, that in the multitude of thy mercies thou hast hitherto spared me.

Accept, I beseech thee, my unfeigned sorrow for my past transgressions; and grant that I may never so presume upon thy mercy, as to despise the riches of thy goodness; but let a sense of thy forbearance and long suffering work in me repentance and amendment of life, to thy honor and glory, and to my final acceptance in the last day, through the merits of my Saviour Jesus Christ.

Keep alive in me, O Lord, a true spirit of devotion; and preserve me from the great sin of praying to thee with my lips only, and not with my heart and mind.

Convince me of my entire dependance upon thee; quicken me in the pursuit of things eternal; that I may continually press forward to obtain the prize of our high calling in Christ Jesus.

Dispose me, I beseech thee, rightly to discharge the duties of this day. Watch over my path; compass me about with thy favor; preserve me in my going out and coming in; and direct all my steps in the way of thy commandments.

Make me truly honest and conscientious in all my dealings; diligent in the performance of my duty; innocent in my conversation; meek, charitable, and forgiving towards others: watchful over myself, and ever mindful of thy presence.

Sanctify unto me my crosses and afflictions, if it be thy good pleasure to afflict me; and give me such a measure of patience and godly resolution, that I may be willing to take up my cross daily, and to follow the Lamb, whithersoever he goeth.

O Lord, if I have now asked any thing amiss, I pray thee pardon my ignorance and infirmity: and whatsoever is good for me, even if I ask it not, be pleased to grant to me, in the name and for the sake of thy dear Son Jesus Christ, our only Mediator and Advocate. Amen.

Our Father, &c.

EVENING PRAYERS.

SUNDAY.

Almighty and most merciful Father, blessed be thy name, that I have again heard the Gospel of thy grace, and the invitations of my Saviour. I adore thee for thy word, which is a light unto my feet, and a lantern to my paths; and, above all, for my hope of peace with thee through the Lamb of God, that taketh away the sin of the world. O make the duties of his Gospel and the calls of his goodness more dear to my heart, that I may glorify him in my body and in my spirit, which are his!

I thank thee, gracious God, for that undeserved compassion which has cast my lot in a Christian land. O make me more anxious to show forth this gratitude, not only with my lips, but in my life, by giving up myself to thy service, and by walking before thee in holiness and righteousness all my days. Teach me, by thy Holy Spirit, that all my means of grace and all my opportunities of salvation must be accounted for in the day of judgment; and that to whom much is given, from them will be much required.

Grant, O merciful God, that the Sabbath now closing may promote thy glory, and set forward the salvation of men, especially of those with whom I have worshipped; that sinners may be converted, and that Christ may see in them of the travail of his soul and be satisfied !

Have mercy, O God of love, upon my relations, and upon all who are near and dear unto me; and give them that godliness which is profitable for all things; which hath the promise of the life that now is, and of that which is to come.

I commend myself to thy merciful protection this night. Be my defence in the hours of sleep and darkness; and if I am permitted to see the light of another day, unite and sanctify my affections to love thee more and serve thee better, for Jesus Christ's sake. Amen.

Our Father, &c.

MONDAY.

O God, my Creator, Preserver, and Benefactor! in the ever adorable name of the Lord Jesus I approach thee with the sincerest reverence and humility, to pay the last acknowledgments of this day to thee, before my eyes are closed with sleep. I praise and magnify thy name for all thy mercies; particularly at this time, for thy preservation of me through the past day, and for that tender care and guidance of thy merciful providence, by which I have been defended from the great and innumerable dangers of soul and body, with which this imperfect state so much abounds. Whatever of good or happiness I enjoy, from thy favor I derive it, and to thee I give the praise. My sinful imperfections and my failings, my transactions and neglects, in many instances, of thy law and my duty, I truly lament, and take the shame of them to myself, humbly beseeching thee to give me true repentance. O forgive me, for thy dear Son's sake, whatsoever thou hast seen amiss in any part of my conduct through the past day, and wash away all my sins in that atoning blood which was shed for sinners. Lord, in mercy take me, and all with whom I am concerned, into thy care and protection through this night. Defend us, if it be thy holy will, from all the designs of evil men, and from everything terrible and hurtful; and lead us all in the paths of holiness, through thy fatherly goodness and love to mankind, declared by thy Son, Jesus Christ our Lord, to whom be glory for ever and ever! Amen.

Our Father, &c.

TUESDAY.

[Hannah More.

O Lord God Almighty, I bless thee for all the mercies of the past day, and I pray thee now to take me under thy care, and to deliver me from all the perils and dangers of this night. Preserve me, O Lord, both in body and soul, from every evil, and keep me from all sinful thoughts when I am about to close my eyes in sleep.

And pardon, I beseech thee, all my offences, for the sake of Jesus Christ. I confess, O Lord, that I have this day left undone many things which I ought to have done, and done many things which I ought not to have done. Pardon all my pride and vanity, my idleness, and self-indulgence, my impatience, fretfulness, and discontent. Pardon, O Lord, all the rash and angry words which I have this day spoken, and all the sinful thoughts which have arisen up in my mind, and which I have not been careful to resist. And especially, I pray thee, to pardon my forgetfulness of thee, my God, and my want of gratitude and love to Jesus Christ. For these and all my other sins which from time to time I have committed, I here implore thy pardon and forgiveness, in the name of my most merciful Saviour.

And, since I know that my life is so short and uncertain, help me, day by day, to think of my latter end. O Lord, grant me grace so to live that I may not be afraid to die: and do thou receive my soul at last into thine eternal kingdom. Amen.

Our Father, &c.

WEDNESDAY.

Almighty and merciful Lord, I praise thee for the mercies of the past day, and I desire to commend myself to thy watchful providence during the silent hours of this night. O thou shepherd of Israel! who never slumberest nor sleepest, watch over me as one of thy flock: embrace, with the arms of thy mercy, and bring into thy fold all my friends and relations, and brethren of mankind, that so, at last, there may be one fold under one shepherd, Jesus Christ.

O Lord, pardon my sins of this day, as well as the sins of my past life, for the sake of him whom thou ladest with the iniquity of us all. May I be daily renewed in the spirit of my mind, by the regenerating influences of the Holy Ghost. May I be enabled to set thee, O Lord, always before mine eyes; trusting in thy gracious promises, and living in humble dependance upon thee. May I receive the blessings of the Father's love, through faith in the finished salvation of the Son.

Hear me, O Lord, for thy mercy is great; and may the words of my mouth, proceeding from the meditation of my heart, be always acceptable in thy sight, through Jesus Christ, my strength, and my Redeemer. Amen.

Our Father, &c.

THURSDAY.

[Bp. Bloomfield.

O Almighty Lord, pardon, I beseech thee, the sins of which I have this day been guilty; consider the weakness of my nature; and, for thy dear Son's sake, be not extreme to mark what is done amiss. I magnify thy goodness, which has so long spared me, and has granted me so much time for repentance; give me grace that I may henceforth turn it to better account.

Enable me, this night, to shake off all worldly cares and desires, and to meditate upon thee; let thy Holy Spirit be present with me in my devotions, to purify my heart, and to bring before me the things which concern my peace, and to inspire me with godly resolutions.

Above all things, make me rightly to understand thine infinite mercy in the redemption of mankind by Jesus Christ, and diligently to avail myself of all my privileges, *as his disciple,* and thy child by adoption and grace.

O heavenly Father, I commit myself to thy holy keeping this night, and desire to rest securely under the shadow of thy protection. Defend me from all perils and dangers, and especially from those which may assault and hurt the soul. Prepare me, by comfortable repose, for the duties of to-morrow; and grant that I may rise disposed and strengthened for thy service as a faithful and diligent disciple of thy blessed Son; in whose words I further pray:

Our Father, &c.

FRIDAY.

In an humble acknowledgment of my manifold sins and iniquities, which I, from time to time, and more especially this day, have committed against Thee, both in thought, word, and deed, I now prostrate myself before thee, O Lord of heaven and earth, beseeching thee for the sake of Jesus Christ, my only Lord and Saviour, to be merciful unto me. Forgive me, O Lord, that I have not rendered unto thee according to thy mercy and loving-kindness; that I have been forgetful and disobedient, and have sinned against heaven and in thy sight. Let thy holy spirit sanctify me throughout, and give me more and more grace and strength, whereby I may be enabled to subdue all my sinful and corrupt affections; grant that I may improve the remainder of my days with all possible care, and give all diligence to make my calling and election sure, that I may so persevere therein unto death, that at last I may attain everlasting life.

Accept my praises and thanksgivings for all thy mercies vouchsafed me in this life, and for the hopes of a better. And now that I am going to take my rest and sleep, let me consider that thou, Lord, only makest me to dwell in safety; whether I sleep or wake, live or die, let me be found thine own, to thy eternal glory, and my everlasting salvation, through Jesus Christ.

Our Father, &c.

SATURDAY.

O MY God, another week has just passed away, and I am still in the land of the living, while so many of my fellow-creatures have passed from time into eternity. Blessed be God for the continuance of life and health, and for prolonged opportunities of preparing for death and judgment.

O gracious God, let not this continuance of mercy increase my condemnation, by encouraging me to commit sin, because hitherto thine anger has been withheld from falling upon me. Let me not treasure up wrath unto myself against the day of wrath; but teach me to number my days, that I may apply my heart unto wisdom.

Prepare me, most blessed God, by sleep and rest, to take my part in the duties of the Sabbath to-morrow. Give me that sense of sin which leads to a full confession of its guilt, and to faith in the atonement of Christ for its pardon. Give me that adoring gratitude for all thy mercies, more especially for the great mercy of a Saviour, which may incline me to praise thee with joyful lips. Give me that sense of the value of my soul, and of the greatness of thy salvation, which may lead me to seek life and mercy with all my heart. O let not the coming Sabbath be defectively used, like those which are passed; but let it be so improved, by public and private means of grace, as to advance my meetness for the service of that eternal

Sabbath that remaineth for the people of God; through the merit and mediation of Jesus Christ. Amen.

Our Father, &c.

SHORT FORMS

FOR MORNING AND EVENING.

These Forms may be added to the following Occasional Prayers, and used instead of the preceding for the Morning or Evening's Devotion.

Morning. (1.)

MERCIFUL and over-looking God, I bless thee for thy care over me the past night. Grant me thy protection through the ensuing day; keep me from all evil; and whatever thou ordainest for me, in small or great events, may I remember that it is thy will, and that I must cheerfully take up my cross to follow the Lord Jesus, my Saviour and Redeemer. Amen.

Our Father, &c.

Morning. (2.)

HEAVENLY Father, Lord God Almighty, I come to thee to implore thine aid and protection through the ensuing day, and to offer thee thanks and praise for all thy mercies, and that of the past night's quiet rest. Make me to walk in thy ways, and so I shall be blessed. Give me the strength to do that which is righteous in thy sight, and may no allurements of gentleness or pleasure wile away my heart from thee.

Make me diligent to do the day's work which is set before me. And in all the trials of hourly existence, the infirmities of my temper and that of others, the crosses and disappointments of worldly hopes and cares, may I, O God, lift up my heart unto thee, through Jesus Christ our Lord. Amen.

Our Father, &c.

Evening. (1.)

Merciful Lord, take me this night under thy kind protection. Watch over me while I sleep. If I wake in the night season, may my meditation of thee be sweet, and my soul be glad in the Lord. If I am spared to see the light of the returning day, may I rise from my bed to give all diligence to walk before thee to all well-pleasing. And whether I wake or sleep, live or die, may I be the Lord's, for Jesus Christ's sake. Amen.

Our Father, &c.

Evening. (2.)

I THANK thee, O Lord, for the blessings which I have this day enjoyed. Grant me this night such refreshing rest, that I may be better able to discharge the duties, and bear the burdens of another day, if thou shalt be pleased to add another day to my life. If my eyes should be kept waking, may my meditations on thee be useful to me. Pity my weakness, O merciful God, and hear my imperfect petitions, for the sake of the Lord Jesus Christ, who is touched with our infirmities, to whom, as to our merciful High Priest, be glory, for ever and ever. Amen.

Our Father, &c.

PRAYERS

FOR VARIOUS OCCASIONS.

PRAYER I.

New-Year's Day.

[Bp. Wilson.

Blessed be God, who has brought me safe to the beginning of another year!

My God, make me truly sensible of this mercy, and give me grace to consider often how short and how uncertain my time is; that there is one year more of a short life passed over my head; and that I am so much nearer eternity:—that I may in good earnest think of another life, and be so prepared for it, as that death may not overtake me unawares.

Lord, pardon all my misspent time, and

make me more diligent and careful to redeem it for the time to come, that when I come to the end of my life, I may look back with comfort on the days that are past.

Grant that I may begin this new year with new resolutions of serving thee more faithfully;—and if, through infidelity or negligence, I forget these good purposes, the good Lord awaken in me a sense of my danger.

My heart is in thy hands, O God, as well as my time; O make me wise unto salvation; that I may consider in this my day the things that belong unto my peace; and that I may pass this, and all the years I have yet to live, in the comfortable hope of a blessed eternity, for the Lord Jesus' sake. Amen.

Our Father, &c.

PRAYER II.

Birth-Day.

[Bp. Wilson.

Blessed be God for my creation and birth; for giving me a being from honest parents fearing God, and in a Christian and Protestant country;—for the means of grace, the assistance of the Holy Spirit, and for the hopes of glory;—for all the known or unobserved favors, providences, and deliverances, by which my life has hitherto been preserved;—most humbly beseeching thee, my God and Father, to pardon my neglect or abuse of any of thy favors, and that I have so very much forgotten thee, in whom I live, and move, and have my being.

Good Lord, forgive me the great waste

of my precious time,—the many days and years of health, and the many opportunities of doing good, which I have lost; and give me grace, that for the time to come I may be truly wise, that I may consider my latter end, and work out my salvation with fear and trembling, ever remembering *the night cometh when no man can work;* and that the day of my death may be better to me than the day of my birth.

O gracious God, grant that before thou takest from me that breath which thou gavest me, I may truly repent of the errors of my past life; that my sins may be forgiven, and my pardon sealed in heaven; when the good Lord shall vouchsafe me a better and an everlasting life through Christ. Amen.

PRAYER III.

Before receiving the Sacrament. (1.)

[Bp. Bloomfield.

ALMIGHTY God, whose blessed Son Jesus Christ, for the forgiveness of our sins, did suffer death upon the cross: prepare me, I beseech thee, by thy grace, for the worthy celebration of that holy ordinance, which he has pleased to appoint for a continual remembrance of his death, for a pledge of his love, and for a sign and means of grace, to my great and endless comfort. Make me to discern the Lord's body: to remember and adore the exceeding love of Christ my Saviour, in thus dying for me. Give me repentance unto life, not to be repented of. Endue me with a lively faith, a perfect love, and a universal charity. Enable me spiritually to receive the body and blood of Christ my Saviour; that so all carnal affections may die in me, and that all things belonging to the Spirit may live and grow in me: and that, being continually refreshed and strengthened by thy grace, I may persevere in all godliness unto my life's end, and finally receive an everlasting recompense, through the merits of Jesus Christ. Amen.

Our Father, &c.

PRAYER IV.

Before receiving the Sacrament. (2.)

[Mrs. Cornwallis.

Almighty God, merciful Father, by whose protection I have been preserved, and by whose clemency I have been spared, grant that the life thou hast prolonged may never be wasted in idleness, nor corrupted by wickedness: let my future purposes be good, and let not my good purposes be vain. Take not from me thy Holy Spirit, but enable me so to commemorate the death of thy dear Son, that I may be made partaker of his merits, and finally for his sake attain everlasting happiness. Grant that this awful remembrance may strengthen my faith; enliven my hope; increase my charity; that I may trust in thee with my whole heart; that I may do thy will with diligence, and suffer it with humble patience; so that, when thou shalt call me to judgment, I may obtain forgiveness and acceptance, for the sake of Jesus Christ, our Saviour. Amen.

Our Father, &c.

PRAYER V.

Confession of Sins.

I ACKNOWLEDGE, dear God, that I have deserved the greatest of thine indignation; that, if thou hadst dealt with me according to my deserts, I should now be bewailing my miseries in a sad eternity; but thy mercy and thy justice triumphing over my sins, thou hast still continued to me time for repentance. Thou hast opened to me the gates of mercy and grace that I might glorify thee. O God, grant that I may at length enter into these gates, and walk hereafter in purity and holiness, by the aid of thy Holy Spirit, through Jesus Christ our Lord. Amen.

Our Father, &c.

PRAYER VI.

For Repentance.

[Bickersteth.

O Thou, who by the right hand of the Father, art called to be a Prince and a Saviour to give repentance and forgiveness of sins, now, in this accepted time, I come to thee, for these great blessings. My heart is hard and impenitent, and little affected by my many sins and thy great goodness; I beseech thee take away the stony heart, and give me a heart of flesh. Vouchsafe unto me that broken and contrite spirit which the High and Holy God will not despise. May thy sufferings, gracious Redeemer, touch and melt my soul. Let the goodness of God lead me to repentance. Never leave me to myself, and my own perverse, wayward, and wandering heart. O now bring me back, by thy Holy Spirit, to my heavenly Father; and returning to him, may I obtain his mercy, and find that he does abundantly pardon, for Jesus Christ's sake. Amen.

Our Father, &c.

PRAYER VII.

For the Pardon of Sin.

[Bp. Taylor.

O Lord, pardon all my sins, my light and rash words, the vanity and impiety of my thoughts, my unjust and uncharitable actions, and whatsoever I have transgressed against thee. Behold, O God, my soul is troubled in the remembrance of my sins, in the frailty and sinfulness of my flesh, exposed to every temptation, and of itself not able to resist any. Lord God of mercy, I earnestly beg of thee to give a great portion of thy grace, such as may be sufficient and effectual for the mortification of all my sins, vanities, and disorders; that, as I have formerly served my lusts and unworthy desires, so now I may give myself up wholly to thy service and the studies of a holy life, through Jesus Christ our Lord. Amen.

Our Father, &c.

PRAYER VIII.

For Faith. (1.)

[Bickersteth.

Almighty God, Father of mercies, from whom cometh every good and perfect gift, give unto me, I beseech thee, grace to believe on the name of Christ. I believe; Lord, help thou my unbelief! let me be strong in faith, giving glory to thee, and having a full persuasion that thou wilt perform all that thou hast promised. O help me to count all things but loss for the excellency of the knowledge of Christ Jesus my Lord. Enable me so to believe, that Christ may dwell in my heart; and I may supremely love thee, my God, and unfeignedly love all my fellow-creatures. Hear me, for Christ's sake. Amen.

Our Father, &c.

PRAYER IX.

For Faith. (2.)

[Mrs. Cornwallis.

O Eternal God, fountain of truth, in whom to believe is life everlasting, let thy grace descend with a mighty power upon my soul. Inspire me with wisdom, knowledge, and humility; and so sanctify my belief in thy revelations, that my heart may be filled with hope and confidence in thy gracious promises. Restrain, O Lord, every vain imagination, and bring every proud thought into subjection to thy will, that no prejudice, no motive of self-interest, may interfere with my full belief in the pure and holy doctrines of Christianity. Hear me, O God, in the name of Jesus Christ. Amen.

Our Father, &c.

PRAYER X

For Strength to resist Temptations.

[Mrs. Cornwallis.

O ALMIGHTY God, the Father of mercies, source of holiness, the fountain of strength, grant me power to resist and overcome all temptations, and to guard against all dangers; that I may not be the slave of accident or violence, of interest or passion, of fear or desire. I am encompassed by infirmities, surrounded by many dangerous allurements; my heart is deceitful, my passions awake, my duties are many and difficult, and my resolutions weak. O be thou unto me wisdom, righteousness, sanctification and redemption. Thou hast promised thy Spirit to those who seek it. Grant that it may dwell with me; instruct, support, and encourage me in holiness, resignation, and every Christian virtue; that I, being ready prepared for every good work, may grow to the full measure of the stature and fulness of thee, my Saviour. Grant that my infirmities may be fewer, and my graces stronger; so that I may walk on stedfastly in the ways of thy laws, and the works of thy commandments; and finally, through the merits and mediation of Jesus Christ, attain to that heavenly kingdom where is fulness of joy and pleasure for evermore. **Amen.**

Our Father, &c.

PRAYER XI.

For Watchfulness against Sin. (1.)

[Bp. Taylor.

TEACH me to watch over all my ways, that I may never be surprised by sudden temptations or a careless spirit, nor return to folly or vanity. Set a watch, O Lord, before my mouth, and keep the door of my lips, that I offend not with my tongue, either against piety or charity. Teach me to think of nothing but thee, and what will promote thy service and glory; to speak of nothing but thee, and thy glories; and to do nothing but what becomes thy servant, whom thine infinite mercy, by the graces of thy Holy Spirit, hath sealed up to the day of redemption.

Let all my passions and affections be so

mortified and brought under the dominion of grace, that I may never, by deliberation and purpose; nor yet by levity, rashness, or inconsideration, offend thy Divine Majesty. Make me such as thou wouldst have me to be; strengthen my faith, confirm my hope, and give me a daily increase of charity, that, this day and ever, I may serve thee according to all my opportunities and capacities, growing from grace to grace; till at last by thy mercies, I shall receive the consummation and perfection of grace in thy kingdom above, through Jesus Christ our Lord. Amen.

Our Father, &c.

PRAYER XII.

For Watchfulness. (2.)

[Dr. Rambach.

O Faithful Saviour! who, like a watchful sheperd, visits thy careful sheep, and warnest them of approaching danger; may I, when inclined to sloth, hear thy pastoral voice sounding in my ears, "Watch and pray." Grant to me a just sense of my inability and weakness, that I may not rely on my own strength or good intentions, but be diligent in prayer for obtaining the succour, and by thy strength may be a conqueror in all things. Amen.

Our Father, &c.

PRAYER XIII.

On reading the Scriptures.

[Bp. Wilson.

O Holy Spirit, make me to understand, embrace, and love the truths of the gospel.

Give, O God, thy blessing unto thy word, that it may become effectual to my conversion and salvation, and to the salvation of all that read and hear it.

Give me grace to read thy Holy Word with the reverence and respect becoming the gracious manifestation of thy will to men; submitting my understanding and will to thine. Let thy gracious promises, O God, contained in thy word, quicken my obedience. Let thy dreadful threatenings and judgments upon sinners make me abhor sin, and lead me to a speedy repentance.

Cause me, O God, to believe thy word, to obey thy commands, to fear thy judgments, and to hope in, and depend upon, thy gracious promises, contained in thy Holy Word, for Jesus Christ's sake.—Amen.

Our Father, &c.

PRAYER XIV.

For Meekness.

[Bp. Wilson.

O Lord, who art a God ready to pardon, slow to anger, and of great kindness, remove far from me all occasions and effects of causeless and immoderate anger; all pride and prejudice, and too much concern for the things of this world;

all intemperate speeches and indecent passions.

Give me, O God, a mild, a peaceable, a meek, and a humble spirit, that remembering my own infirmities, I may bear with those of others:—that I may think lowly of myself, and not be angry when others also think lowly of me; that I may be patient towards all men; gentle and easy to be entreated, that God, for Christ's sake, may be so towards me. Amen.

Our Father, &c.

PRAYER XV.

For Spiritualized Affections.

[Bp. Ken.

O Lord, enlighten my understanding, that I may know Thee; sanctify my affections, that I may love Thee; and put thy fear into my heart, that I may dread to offend Thee.

Wean my affections, O Lord, from the things of this world, and whatever my state and condition may be here, give me grace therewith to be content.

O my God! let the consideration of the emptiness of pleasure, the troubles and miseries of riches, and the shortness and vanity of all things in the world, inspire me with due contempt of all enjoyments here below; and make me ever shun these hindrances to a life of holiness and virtue, that I may with the greater freedom enjoy thee, O my God! in meditating on thy perfections and thy glories. Let me, dearest Jesus, have those influences of thy blessed Spirit in my retirements, that I may at last grow wholly weary of the world, and then fix my thoughts upon that heavenly kingdom, where true pleasures, fulness of riches, and lasting honors, are only to be met withal; whither let thy mercy speedily bring me, that I may be satisfied with the fulness of thy presence, and meditate for ever on thy great perfections, joining with all the glorious attendants on thy throne in endless songs of thy eternal praises. Amen.

Our Father, &c.

PRAYER XVI.

For Holiness. (1.)

O MY God, thou art of purer eyes than to behold iniquity, neither shall sinners dwell in thy sight. Only the pure in heart are blessed; for only they shall see God.

Mortify the love, and overcome the power, of iniquity within me. Make my body the temple of the Holy Ghost, a habitation of God through the Spirit. O let me come out from the ways and practice of sin; let me not touch the unclean thing, that thou mayest be a Father unto me, and that I may be the child of thy love, and the heir of thy bliss, through Jesus Christ. Amen.

Our Father, &c.

PRAYER XVII.

For Holiness. (2.)

O Heavenly Father, help me to cast off the works of darkness, and put on the armour of light. I would walk in the light, as thou art in the light: but my desires are faint, my wishes feeble, my resolutions transient as the morning cloud, or as the early dew; temptation overtakes me, and sin subdues me. Have compassion upon thy servant, O Lord, and deal with me according to the greatness of thy mercy.

Withdraw not thy Holy Spirit from me, although I have so little improved its blessed influences, or followed its heavenly guidance, in time past. Thou alone canst restore my soul. Into thy hands I commit it. Wash it from all guilt, in the fountain open for sin and for uncleanness; sanctify it wholly to thyself; let not sin have dominion over me: beat down Satan under my feet; strengthen me to run the way of thy commandments, and so shall I rejoice in thy great salvation, through Jesus Christ. Amen.

Our Father, &c.

PRAYER XVIII.

Against Wandering Thoughts in Prayer.

[Bp. Wilson.

O HOLY Spirit of grace, help my infirmities, that I may fix my thoughts upon my duty; and that I may serve Thee with all my heart and mind:—that I may never give way to wandering thoughts, but watch against them continually.

Look upon me, O Lord, and pity me; make me and let me be thine, by the choice of my will; make me serious and thoughtful at all times, that I may not fail being so when I attend upon God.

Let not my heart, O God, be inclined to any evil thing. Keep me, O God, fiom every thing that may displease Thee ; and make me wise unto salvation, for Jesus Christ's sake. Amen.

Our Father, &c.

PRAYER XIX.

For a Right Use of Time.

Almighty God, I adore thy infinite patience, which hath not cut me off in the midst of my follies : I magnify thy wonderful goodness, which hath spared me thus long, and indulged me with a larger time of repentance. Let me no longer abuse that precious treasure, which thou hast allotted me as a proper season to work out my own salvation, and secure that happiness which is great in itself, and infinite in its duration.

Let me bid adieu to all those vain amusements, those trifling entertainments and sinful diversions, which have robbed me of many valuable hours, and endangered the loss of my immortal soul. Let me no longer waste my time in ease and pleasure, in unprofitable studies, and more unprofitable conversation; but grant, that by diligence and honesty in my calling, by constancy and fervor in my devotions, by moderation and temperance in my enjoyments, by justice and charity in all my words and actions, and by keeping a conscience void of offence to God and man, I may be able to give a good account of it in the day of judgment and be accepted in and through the merits of Jesus Christ, my only mediator and advocate. Amen.

Our Father, &c.

PRAYER XX.

For God's Direction.

O God, who seest I have no power of myself, that I am not wise enough for my own direction, nor strong enough for my own defence; let me acknowledge thee in all my ways, and not lean to my own understanding. Let thy light guide me, thy providence protect me, thy grace enable me that I may faithfully discharge all the public and private duties thou shalt think fit to call me to; that, being thus armed with thy defence, I may be preserved from all dangers, through Jesus Christ our Lord. Amen.

Our Father, &c.

PRAYER XXI.

For Humility.

[Bp. Taylor.

O Lord God, who resists the proud, and givest grace to the humble; endue me with such humility of soul, and modesty of behavior, that my looks may not be proud, my thoughts arrogant, nor my designs ambitious; but that being restrained of all vanity and pride, and my affections weaned from a great opinion and love of myself, I may trust in thee, follow the example of my blessed Master, and receive those promises thou hast made in our Lord and Saviour Jesus Christ.—Amen.

Our Father, &c.

PRAYER XXII.

For the Love of God.

O Thou infinite goodness and love, be thou pleased to pardon all the defects of my love to thee, and all the excesses of my love to earthly things; and turn my inclinations and affections from all vain objects to thy blessed self, who art the worthiest of all love; and to conquer all my prejudice, and forever win my heart. O show thyself to me as a pardoning God; full of compasion, ready to forgive, and willing to save me. Yea, make me to know so much of the love wherewith thou hast loved me, that I may make better returns of love to the gracious giver of all my good. Touch my heart with such a powerful sense of thy loveliness and loving-kindness, that I may experience stronger desires and inclinations after thee, and greater complacence and delight in thee; and may I love all other things, in comparison of my best and dearest Lord, as if I loved them not.—Enable me, by thy good help and grace, to keep myself in the love of God, looking for the mercy of our Lord Jesus Christ to eternal life. Amen.

Our Father, &c.

PRAYER XXIII.

For Patience under Afflictions. (1.)

[Author of the Retrospect.

O my heavenly Father! enable me in all my trials and afflictions to lie passive in thy hands; pardon thou my unbecoming fears, and strengthen the faith of thy wavering servant; compassionate my many and great frailties, and cheer my heart in the hour of despondency; let a well-grounded hope of thy love and mercy be imparted under every conflict, and a prospect of heaven be afforded amidst all the sorrows and darkness of these wilderness scenes.

Lord! I trust I am thine: save me, and sanctify me by every event and visitation which I am called to experience, while passing through a world of sorrow, sin, and death. And whether I live or die, may I be the Lord's. Amen.

Our Father, &c.

PRAYER XXIV.

For Patience under Afflictions. (2.)

[Dr. Rambach.

Gracious God, my sufferings are great, but not to be compared to those of my Saviour; yet I know that even the hours of my sufferings are limited by thy providence, and thou countest them to me. Thou appointest their beginning and end. Grant that I may acquiesce with my whole heart in what thou art pleased to inflict, who orderest every thing for the good of thy creatures. Thou wilt not only limit the period of my sufferings, but wilt never suffer me to be tempted above what I am able to bear. Preserve me, O Lord, from the gloom of unbelief, from the darkness of spiritual blindness, and from the eternal night or the dark abyss. Sanctify to me every pain and every sorrow, that I may pass through the furnace of affliction, as gold purified in the fire; and when I have suffered all thou hast appointed unto me, may I come off more than a conqueror, through him that hath loved me and given himself for me. Amen.

Our Father, &c.

PRAYER XXV.

Under Spiritual Trouble.

SAVE me, O God, for the waters are come into my soul: I sink in the deep mire where there is no standing. Bring my soul out of prison, that I may praise thy name.

O show me the true estate of my soul, and make me to know the things that are freely given of God; and deliver me, gracious Lord, from all those offensive matters that provoke thee to hide thy face from me, and that wrap up my soul in clouds and darkness, and make me so much a stranger to peace and comforts. O grant me a clear discovery of the evidences of my calling and election; and seal a comfortable assurance of thy blessed love in Christ Jesus to my soul. O thou who didst bid the winds and waves, Peace, be still, and they obeyed thee,—settle my discomposed mind, and quiet my troubled breast, and bring me to see the light of thy countenance, and the joy of thy salvation. O thou who art of power to establish us, be pleased to establish my heart with grace, and let me be rooted and grounded in the faith, that I may not stagger, through unbelief, but hold the beginning of my confidence steadfast unto the end. Rejoice the soul of thy servant; for unto thee, O Lord, do I lift up my soul; and let the joy of the Lord be my strength, to make me victorious over my sins, and always to abound in thy work; never pleased so much with any thing as to do the things pleasing to my God, through Jesus Christ. Amen.

Our Father, &c.

PRAYER XXVI.

An Invocation to the Holy Spirit.

[Author of the Retrospect.

Oh, thou Holy Spirit! whose delight it is to convince sinners of their need of a Redeemer, and then lead them unto Christ and give them faith to believe, do thou evermore dwell in my heart, and keep me ever mindful of my wants, and humbled for my sins. Give me, O thou Comforter and Sanctifier, give me grace to apply all his blessed work of redemption, all his gracious promises, to my soul. Enable me, as in the presence of a heart-searching God, day by day to declare, that this Saviour is my all, my theme, my inspiration, and my crown. Nothing short of this exceeding riches of grace, this incomprehensible weight of glory, can satisfy my soul. Oh! give me Christ, or all other gifts will be worse than nothing. Without Christ, life would be the prelude to certain and eternal death, and existence itself the greatest of curses.

Come, thou Eternal, Holy Spirit! come and possess this soul of mine, and consecrate all its faculties to the service and glory of the Eternal Jevohah, forever and and forever. Amen.

Our Father, &c.

PRAYER XXVII.

For the Graces of the Spirit.

[Author of the Retrospect.

O Almighty, blessed, and eternal God, I now come, and in the name of Him in whom thou art well-pleased, I ask for grace to keep me in all my ways; for wisdom to instruct and direct me in all my wanderings and ignorance; for courage to confess Christ before men; for all those fruits and graces of thy Spirit, which shall enable me to glorify thy name in the world and to serve my fellow-creatures for their good, until I am gathered to my fathers and see corruption. And when the enemy comes in with the power of an overwhelming flood, the subtlety of hell, or in the garb of an angel of light, do thou stand by me and deliver my soul. When pain and sickness try this mortal body, do thou impart the meekness and resignation of a lamb unto my spirit. When death itself approaches, and the solemn scenes of eternity unfold themselves to my view, do thou enable me to read my title clear to a habitation not made with hands, eternal in the heavens; for Jesus Christ's sake. Amen.

Our Father, &c.

PRAYER XXVIII.

Gratitude to God for Spiritual Blessings.

[Author of the Retrospect.

What shall I render unto thee, O my God! for all thy mercies! Aid me with thine own Spirit to offer up all the gratitude and praise which a poor heart like mine is capable of. Yes, I will praise thy holy name, for making me willing, in the day of thy power, to come out from the ambitious, restless pursuits of men, who desire their good things here. I adore thee for showing me the vanity and danger of seeking my portion on earth, and the madness of expecting happiness in the paths of the destroyer. How many of my competitors and companions in the race of sin and vanity have stumbled, and fallen, and perished! Still I am among the living to praise thee! Hence, O Lord, let me seek and find all my repose and all my happiness in thee. Whatever comforts thou art pleased to communicate through the medium of thy creatures to my body, and whatever refreshments may be supplied through ordinances and means of grace to my soul, still, O my God, may I see and receive all as coming from thee, through Jesus Christ. Amen.

Our Father, &c.

PRAYER XXIX.

Before going a Journey.

O Lord, thou art the same God in all places: and no where can I go but thou art there. Both at home and abroad, on my way and at the end, thou art ever with me by the universal presence of thy grace, and thy good Spirit with me, to conduct and guide me continually; to protect and save me from all dangers and mischiefs; and to make my way prosperous, and all my affairs successful. O let the blessing of the Lord follow me, and rest upon me; and preserve my going out, and my coming in; and never leave me, nor forsake me, O Lord, but be my God and guide this day in all this journey, and all my life long; which is but a pilgrimage and passage through this world, in which I am continually hastening home, to the period of all my travels, to the place where I must take up my abode and dwell forever. Amen.

Our Father, &c.

PRAYER XXX.

For the Spread of the Gospel.

O FATHER of lights, and giver of all wisdom, bless every society formed for the conversion of Jews or Gentiles, and for the spread and advancement of thy truth, at home or abroad.

Look with favor on all missionaries now among the heathen. O prepare thy way in the wilderness. May every valley be exalted, and every hill be made low; may the crooked be made straight, and the rough places plain; and let thy word have free course every where and be glorified. May thy doctrine, constantly preached by thy servants, drop as the rain, and distil as the dew, and thy word never return unto thee void, but prosper abundantly, and accomplish all that for which thou dost send it. Give thy servants health and strength, vigor of mind, and devotedness of heart; and may they all be chosen vessels to bear thy name before the Gentiles. May the deadening influence of climate, heathen customs, and loss of means of grace, be more than counteracted by a special supply of thy Holy Spirit. Give them grace to be faithful unto death, and may they receive from the Saviour's hands the crown of life and glory. Grant that thousands and tens of thousands may rise up to call thee blessed. May the little leaven leaven the whole lump: and all nations whom thou hast made, fall down and worship before thee, and glorify thy name, through thy dear Son. Amen.

Our Father, &c.

PRAYER XXXI.

For Resignation to the Divine Will.

Pascal.

O Lord, take from me that sorrow which the love of self may produce from my sufferings, and from my unsuccessful hopes and designs in this world, while regardless of thy glory; but create in me a sorrow resembling thine. Let me not henceforth desire health or life, except to spend them for thee, with thee, and in thee. I pray not that thou wouldst give me either health or sickness, life or death: but that thou wouldst dispose of my health and my sickness, my life and my death, for thy glory, for my own eternal welfare, for the use of the church, and the benefit of thy saints, of whose number, by thy grace, I hope to be. Thou alone knowest what is good for me; thou art Lord of all; do, therefore, what seemeth thee best. Give to me, or take from me; conform my will to thine; and grant that with humble and perfect submission, and in holy confidence, I may be disposed to receive the orders of thy eternal providence; and may equally adore every dispensation, which will come to me from thy hand, through Jesus Christ our Lord. Amen.

Our Father, &c.

PRAYER XXXII.

In the prospect of Death.

Bp. Wilson.

In my last hour, O Lord, I humbly beg thy protection from the busy suggestions of evil spirits. O let not my faith fail, my hope wither, or my charity wax cold with the waning flesh; but when mine eyes are darkened, and my tongue falters, then, O then, let my heart be enlarged towards thee, waiting on thee, longing for thee incessantly, and praying, Show me thy mercy, O Lord, and grant me thy salvation. Since my days are but as a span, short and uncertain, I humbly beseech thee, O Lord, to wean my heart from the disquietudes of worldly cares, that I may be diligent in all the good works of obedience and charity, that so, recovering the spiritual health of my soul, I may die in thy grace and favor, through Jesus Christ.

Our Father, &c.

EJACULATIONS,

CHIEFLY FROM THE SCRIPTURES.

In the Morning.

What shall I offer unto the Lord for his mercies renewed unto me every morning! The sacrifice of God is a broken spirit: a broken and a contrite heart, O God, thou wilt not despise.

Grant that I may continue in thy fear all the day long. May I keep thy statutes and observe thy laws.

Be with me this day in my going out and in my coming in. Make me watchful and circumspect in my walk and conversation. Put thy fear in my heart, O God, that I may be kept from sinning against thee.

In Conversation.

Set a watch, O Lord, before my mouth; keep thou the door of my lips.

Let the words of my mouth and the meditation of my heart, be always acceptable in thy sight, O Lord, my Strength and my Redeemer.

Preserve me, O God, from a vain conversation; give me grace never to be ashamed or afraid to speak of Thee and Thy law.

In Temptation.

When the enemy comes in like a flood, do thou, the Spirit of the Lord, lift up a standard against him; enable me to stand in the evil day, and having done all, to stand.

How can I do this great wickedness and sin against God?

Against any besetting Sin.

ENABLE me to lay aside every weight, and the sin that doth most easily beset me; and to run with patience the race that is set before me, looking unto Jesus.

On falling into Sin.

HAVE mercy upon me, O God, and according to the multitude of thy tender mercies, blot out my transgressions. Wash me thoroughly from mine iniquity, and cleanse me from my sin, hide thy face from my sins, and blot out mine iniquities.

When Evil Entreated.

Give me, O my God, a heart full of Christian meekness and charity, that I may willingly forget the evil I have received, and be always disposed to do good to others.

In difficult Circumstances.

I will lift up my eyes unto the hills, from whence cometh my help. Hear my prayers, O Lord, and let my cry come unto thee. Hide not thy face from me in the time of my trouble.

Cause me to know the way wherein I should walk; for I lift up my soul unto thee.

Lord, I am oppressed; undertake for me. In all my ways may I acknowledge thee; and do thou in mercy direct my path.

At Self-Examination.

Examine me, O Lord, and prove me; try thou my reins and my heart.

Search me, O God, and know my heart: try me, and know my thoughts; and see if there be any wicked way in me; and lead me in the way everlasting.

On any Loss.

The Lord gave, and the Lord hath taken away; blessed be the name of the Lord.

It is the Lord, let him do what seemeth him good. Enable me to bear patiently whatever trials may be allotted me, firmly trusting in thy word, that all things shall work together for good to them that love thee

In Trouble of Mind.

When my heart is overwhelmed within me, lead me to the Rock that is higher than I. Why art thou cast down, O my soul; and why art thou disquieted within me; Hope thou in God; for I shall yet praise Him, who is the health of my countenance and my God.

Before Prayer.

Lord, teach me to pray. Quicken me that I may call upon thy name.

Before Reading the Scriptures.

Open thou mine eyes, that I may behold wondrous things out of thy law.

Sanctify me through thy truth; thy word is truth.

On Going to Church.

How amiable are thy tabernacles, O Lord of Hosts! My soul longeth, yea, my heart and my flesh crieth out for the living God.

On Going to Bed.

I WILL lay me down in peace, and take my rest; for it is thou, Lord, only that makest me to dwell in safety.

DEVOUT MEDITATIONS.

MEDITATION I.

On Communion with God in Secret.

[Bp. Ken.

Retire, O my soul! from the busy world, and employ thyself about that for which thou wert created:—The contemplation of thy God. I will hasten to my closet, or yonder solitary walk, and there sequestered from a vexatious world, I will not suffer a single thought of it to approach me, unless by way of pity and contempt.

How delightful is it, O my soul! for thee to enjoy this sweet communion with thy God, and thus to dwell upon divine objects. Here am I safe, and at rest, in this dear place of quiet; and earnestly pity all the men of business and hurry, whose heads are full of perplexing contrivances, to procure a little happiness in a world where there is no such thing.

O blessed freedom! O charming solitude! I will grasp you, and I will hold you fast—the delight of silence and retreat! Here I can unburthen my soul, and pour it out before my God. Here I can wrestle with the powers of heaven, and not let them go till I have obtained a blessing. Here I can confess my sins, and with hopes of comfort lay open my troubled breast before the merciful Hearer of my prayers.

cross of Christ, seen by faith, will enable you to crucify the world. It will bring you pardon and victory. It will engage you in another cause, occupy you with other objects, and introduce you into other society. It will detect all the glare and imposition of earthly things. The mysterious death of the incarnate Saviour will fix your heart, produce hatred of sin, reconcile you to reproach, deliver you from the fear of man, and make obedience delightful.

MEDITATION XI.

On Prayer.

O MY soul! what canst thou desire beyond this? Ask whatsoever thou wilt in the name of Jesus, and in the faith of his holy word; and if it be for the glory of God, and the real good of thy soul, thou shalt as surely have thy request granted, as that the Lord Jehovah liveth, and answereth prayer.—*Author of the Retrospect.*

O Lord, I know not what I should ask of thee. Thou only knowest what I want; and thou lovest me better than I can love myself. O Lord, give to me, who desires to be thy child, what is proper, whatsoever it may be. I dare not ask either crosses or comforts. I only present myself before thee; I open my heart to thee. Behold my wants, which I am ignorant of: but do thou behold, and do according to thy mercy. Smite or heal; depress or raise me up: I adore all thy purposes, without knowing them: I am silent, I offer myself in sacrifice. I abandon myself to thee, having no greater desire than to accomplish thy will. Teach me to pray. Pray thou myself in me.—*Abp. Fenelon.*

MEDITATION XII.

On the Sufferings of Christ.

[Scott.

Once more, O my soul! let thy meditations turn for a moment on the complicated cruelties and indignities to which the holy and spotless Lamb of God was exposed. He was wounded and scourged, that thou mightest be healed. He was arrayed with scorn in the purple robe, that he might procure for thee the robe of righteousness and salvation. He was crowned with thorns, that thou mightest be crowned with honor and immortality. He stood speechless that thou mightest have an all-prevailing plea. He endured torture, that thou mightest have a strong consolation. He thirsted, that thou mightest drink of the waters of life.— He bore the wrath of the Father, that thou mightest enjoy his favor. He was numbered with transgressors, that thou mightest be made equal with the angels. He died, that thou mightest live for ever! Oh! then, let me often retire and meditate on this scene, and admire his immeasureable love, that I may learn to mourn for sin, and hate it, and rejoice in my obligations to such a Redeemer, until I am constrained to live no longer unto myself, but to him who died for me, and rose again.

MEDITATION XIII.

On Death.

[Cæsar Malan.

We were born, and we must die. The time allotted to us here below is short indeed. If we stretch out our hands, we may almost touch the portals which terminate the path of our mortal pilgrimage. If we listen with attention, we seem to hear the labor of him who is engaged in preparing our graves; and, if the Holy Spirit is pleased to open our ears, we may already discern the sounds which proceed from the celestial abodes.

Listen, O my soul, to this warning voice with the deepest attention! "All flesh is grass, and the glory of man is as the flower of the field." Fresh and verdant in the morning, it adorns the meadow: the sight is gladdened at its beauty, and it sheds sweet perfumes around. "In the evening it is cut down and withered!" Its glory is departed; and it tells us that a few hours must suffice for earthly enjoyments. The day is passed—the grass and the flowers thereof are gone.

MEDITATION XIV.

On the Joys of Heaven.

[Bp. Ken.

HAIL, the despised followers of the poverty of Jesus! he had no estates,—he had no purchase on earth, not "a hole wherein to lay his sacred head." In this you were like your suffering Lord; for your treasures were in heaven, where you now enjoy them with an assurance of an everlasting possession; you are now no longer heirs but actual inheritors of that kingdom of inexpressible wealth, from which he has utterly debarred all that are encumbered with riches here below, and place their security and reliance on them. What divine melody is this, O my soul, which thus charms my ravished thoughts? What vigorous echoes of joy inexpressible are these I hear? These can be none other than the voices of angels. Oh, the fervor of this joy! as if their heavenly breasts were unable to contain the flaming zeal within. Lo! how they break forth into the most ardent expressions, and pathetic hallelujahs to your Creator's glory! Hark! what heavenly song is this I hear?

"Holy, holy, holy, Lord God Almighty! which was, and is, and is to come. Blessing, honor, power, and glory, be unto him that sitteth upon the throne, and to the Lamb, for ever and ever!"

SELF-EXAMINATION.

Examine yourselves whether ye be in the faith; prove your own selves.—2 Cor. xiii. 5.

It is only by scrutinizing the heart that we can know it. It is only by knowing the heart that we can reform the life. Any careless observer indeed, when his watch goes wrong, may see that it does so by casting an eye on the dial plate; but it is only the artist who takes it to pieces and examines every spring and every wheel separately, and who, by ascertaining the precise causes of the irregularity, can set the machine right, and restore the obstructed movements. Dr. Barrow has remarked, that "it is a peculiar excellency of human nature, and which distinguishes man from the inferior creatures more than bare reason itself, that he can reflect upon all that is done within him, can discern the tendencies of his soul, and is acquainted with his own purposes."

Nothing more plainly shows us what weak, vascillating creatures we are, than the difficulty we find in fixing ourselves down to the very self-scrutiny we had deliberately resolved on. Like the worthless Roman emperor, we retire to our closet under the appearance of serious occupation, but might now and then be surprised, if not in catching flies, yet in pursuits nearly as contemptible. Some trifle which we should be ashamed to dwell upon at any time, intrudes itself on the moments dedicated to serious thought; recollection is interrupted; the whole chain of reflection broken, so that the scattered links cannot again be united. And so inconsistent are we, that we are sometimes not sorry to have a plausible pretence for interrupting the very employment in which we had just before made it a duty to engage. For want of this home acquaintance, we remain in utter ignorance of our inability to meet even the ordinary trials of life with cheerfulness; indeed by this neglect we confirm that inability.

We have appetites to control, imaginations to restrain, tempers to regulate, passions to subdue; and how can this internal work be effected, how can our thoughts be kept within due bounds, how can a proper bias be given to the affections, how can the little state of man be preserved from continual insurrection, how can this restraining power be maintained, if this capacity of discerning, if this faculty of inspecting be not kept in regular exercise? Without constant discipline, imagination will become outlaw, conscience an attainted rebel.

This inward eye, this power of introversion, is given us for a continual watch upon the soul. On an unremitted vigilance over its interior motions, those fruitful seeds of action, those prolific principles of vice and virtue, will depend both the formation and the growth of our moral and religious character. A superficial glance is not enough for a thing so deep, an unsteady view will not suffice for a thing so wavering, nor a casual look for a thing so deceitful as the human heart. A partial inspection on any one side, will not be enough for an object which must be observed under a variety of aspects, because it is always shifting its positions, always changing its appearances.

We should examine not only our conduct but our opinions ; not only our faults but our prejudices ; not only our propensities but our judgments. Our actions themselves will be obvious enough ; it is our intentions which require the scrutiny. These we should follow up to their remotest springs, scrutinize to their deepest recesses, trace through their most perplexing windings. And lest we should in our pursuit wander in uncertainty and blindness, let us make use of that guiding clue, as furnished by his word, and by his Spirit, for conducting us through the intricacies of this labyrinth. What I know not teach thou me, should be our constant petition in all our researches.*

Nor must the examination be occasional, but regular. Let us not run into long arrears, but settle our accounts frequently. Little articles will run up to a large amount, if they are not cleared off. Even our *innocent* days, as we may choose to call them, will not have passed without furnishing their contingent—our deadness in devotion—our eagerness for human applause—our care to conceal our faults rather than to correct them—our negligent performance of some relative duty—our imprudence in conversation, especially

* Vide Practical Piety, Vol. i.

at table—our inconsideration—our driving to the very edge of permitted indulgences; —let us keep these—let us keep all our numerous items in small sums. Let us examine them while the particulars are fresh in our memory; otherwise however we may flatter ourselves that lesser evils will be swallowed up by the greater, we may find when we come to settle the grand account, that they will not be the less remembered for not having been recorded.

In the discharge of this necessary and important duty, the Christian should remember that every day he lives he has

A God to Glorify.—1 COR. VI. 20.

A Soul to Save.—PHIL. ii. 12, 13.

Repentance to seek and perform.—ACTS v. 31. LUKE xiii. 3.

A Saviour to believe and imitate.—ACTS xvi. 31. 1 PET. ii. 21.

A Body to mortify through the Spirit.—ROM viii. 13.

Graces and Virtues to implore by earnest Prayer.—PHIL. iv. 6. MARK xi. 24.

Sins to weep over and forsake.—LUKE vii. 38. PROV. xxviii. 13.

Mercies and Deliverances to remember.—PSAL. lvi. 12, 13. PSAL. ciii. 1, 4.

A Hell to avoid.—MATT. iii. 7. PSAL. ix. 17.

A Paradise to gain.—REV. ii. 7, 10.

An Eternity to meditate on.—COLOSS. iii. 2.

Time to redeem.—EPHES. v. 16.

A Neighbor to edify.—ROM. xv. 2. LUKE xxii. 32.

Works of Charity to perform.—MATT. xxv. 40.

A World to fear and yet to conquer.—2. COR. vi. 17. 1 JOHN v. 4.

Devils to combat.—EPH vi. 12.

Passions to subdue.—2 COR. x . 5. EPH. iv. 31, 32.

And, PERHAPS, Death to suffer.—LUKE xii. 20.

And Judgment to undergo.—2 COR. v. 10.

And all these must be met and performed in

the GRACE OF CHRIST, and not in your own strength, which is perfect weakness.—2 COR. xiii. 10. PHIL. iv. 13.

There is a spurious sort of self-examination, which does not serve to enlighten but to blind. A person who has left off some notorious vice, who has softened some shades of a glaring sin, or substituted some outward forms in the place of open religion, looks on his change of character with pleasure. He compares himself with what he was, and views the alteration with self-complacency. He deceives himself by taking his standard from his former conduct, or from the character of still worse men, instead of taking it from the unerring rule of Scripture. He looks rather at the discredit than the sinfulness of his former life, and being more ashamed at what is disreputable than grieved at what is vicious, he is, in this state of shallow reformation, more in danger in proportion as he is more in credit. He is not aware that it is not having a fault or two less that will carry him to heaven, while his heart is still glued to the world and estranged from God.

How necessary then it is that the Christian should minutely examine his motives and actions—that he should constantly say, with the Royal Psalmist,—"Search me, O God, and know my heart; try me, and know my thoughts; and see if there be any wicked way in me, and lead me in the way everlasting." In discharging this duty, the Christian will be greatly assisted, by attending to the following simple rules:—

I. *Let a fixed time be set apart every morning and evening for this purpose.*

It is impossible to give any rule as to the length of time that should be given. The obligations of persons vary with their situations and circumstances; but let us give as much time, as, consistently with our other duties, we can spare, and let the time in every case be so employed, not as a task, but as a blessing; not merely as a requirement, but as a privilege and advantage; for the more close, faithful, and diligent you are in self-examination, the more comfort and benefit you are likely to receive in the end.

II. *Consider the Holy Scriptures as the great test by which you are to try yourself.*

They are the only true standard of self-examination—the touchstone which discovers at once the character of the metal; and by comparing your state with the most practical and spiritual parts of God's word, and varying those parts from time to time, you try yourself by a perfect and infallible standard.

III. *Conduct this examination in the spirit of Prayer.*

Prayer is the guide to self-knowledge, by prompting us to look after our sins, in order to pray against them; it is a motive to vigilance by teaching us to guard against those sins, which, through self-examination, we have been enabled to detect.

IV. *Beware of formality and self-righteousness.*

Although it is our unbounden duty to guard against the commission of sin, and to keep ourselves unspotted from the world, yet it is not our watchfulness against sin, or our performance of any religious duty, however good in itself, which constitutes us genuine Christians. For after all we have done or can do, we are but unprofitable servants. We should hate sin, because it is hateful in the sight of God, we should seek to be delivered from its dominion by earnest prayer, and depend alone for salvation on the merits and righteousness of the Lord Jesus Christ, who is emphatically styled the Lord our Righteousness; for all dependance upon our own good works will only prove a means of delusion and danger to our souls.

A PRAYER BEFORE SELF-EXAMINATION.

Holy, holy, Lord God Almighty, who art of purer eyes than to behold iniquity, who searchest the heart and triest the innermost thoughts, I beseech thee now to assist me in looking into my own heart, and my own life. Feeling and acknowledging that my heart is deceitful above all things, and desperately wicked, I beseech thee to show me to myself. Enable me to try myself by the standard of thy holy word, and discover the true state of my soul; give me repentance for all my past sins, lively faith in Jesus Christ the only Saviour from sin, deep humility before thee, and such tempers and dispositions as are meet for those who assemble round the table of our gracious Redeemer. These things I ask for his name's sake.

QUESTIONS FOR SELF-EXAMINATION.

Morning.

1. Have I this morning sought of the Lord his special grace and protection for the day?

2. Am I going forth in my own strength, or simply looking to God alone to help and deliver?

3. Am I so sensible of my own weakness as ever to watch and pray?

4. Am I living by faith in a daily and simple dependance on God?

5. Do I constantly remember that I am accountable to God for a right improvement of the talents entrusted to me?

6. Have I determined to lay myself out this day for the glory of God?

7. Are all the faculties of my soul engaged to

render affectionate, intelligent, sincere, and resolute service?

8. Have I resolved, in the strength of God, to forsake all sins, however dear to me, particularly my besetting sin, whether it be pride, envy, malice, covetousness, impurity, fear of man, or any other sin?

9. Is it my constant desire to abstain from, the very appearance of evil, and to keep myself unspotted from the world?

Evening.

1. Did I this morning make my resolutions to walk closely with God, in dependance on his gracious assistance?

2. Have I this day put up petitions against my besetting sins?

3. What have I committed, and what omitted, to-day?

4. What mercies have I received this day—

Answers to prayer—Deliverance from evil—Common or remarkable blessings?

5. What have I done this day for the glory of God or the good of my fellow-creatures; or what opportunities have I neglected of promoting them?

6. Have I been enabled this day willingly to take up my cross?

7. Have I been watching to-day against the first risings of pride and wordly-mindedness?—Have I guarded against the appearance of evil?

8. Have I kept up a lively and humble dependance upon the Divine influence, in the duty and emergencies of the day?

9. With what success have I encountered the sins to which my circumstances or constitution most incline me?

10. Have I been looking to Jesus as my righteousness, my strength, and my example?

11. How have I improved my time this day?—Have I made any progress in religion?—Have

I thought of Death and Judgment?—Have I walked with God?

12. Have I this day tried to mortify sin?

13. Have I prayed, and how?—Have I read the Scriptures, and how?

General Questions.

1. Do I think much and frequently of God, and am I zealous for his glory?

2. Do I enjoy communion with God when I pray to him, or desire this?

3. Do I strive to become like him?

4. Am I actively desiring and seeking the good of all, around me, even as I desire my own?

5. Is my love to others like that of Christ to me?

6. Have the miseries of others called forth compassion and efforts to relieve them?

7. Am I seeking the salvation of my fellow-creatures?

8. Is sin hateful to me?—Do I loathe it as the worst of all evils?

9. Have I an habitual mourning for sin?

10. Have I deeply felt my corruption and guilt before God?

11. Do I believe that the Gospel is the appointed and only complete way of salvation?

12. Do I rest on the only hope of forgiveness—redemption through the blood of Christ?

13. Am I so believing in Jesus as to rely upon him as my Saviour?

14. Am I truly grateful to God for his great salvation?

15. Am I evidencing this by a care to please him in all things?

16. Am I humble and lowly in mind, affection, and conversation?

17. Do the sufferings of Christ for sin affect my heart with godly sorrow?

18. Am I patient under crosses, trials, and injuries, and willing to suffer reproach for Christ's sake?

19. Do I quietly submit to God's painful dispensations?

20. Do I hunger and thirst after righteousness?

21. Do I earnestly desire to obtain that righteousness which is through the faith of Christ?

22. Am I laboring to spread the Gospel of Peace?

23. Do I seek to know God more myself, and to diffuse his knowledge through the world?

24. Have I resigned myself to the will of God, to do and suffer his pleasure?

25. How do I spend my Sabbaths?—Do I not in too many instances employ these opportunities of mercy in unprofitable and sinful conversation; in doing many unnecessary works; by travelling, visiting, &c., instead of improving them, so as to promote the glory of God and my own spiritual advantage?

RESOLUTIONS.*

1. Resolved, that *I will do whatever* I think to be most to God's glory and my own good, profit and pleasure, ON THE WHOLE, without any consideration of the time, whether now, or never so many myriads of ages hence: to do whatever I think to be my *duty*, and most for the good and advantage of mankind in general —whatever difficulties I meet with, how many and how great soever.

2. Resolved, to be continually endeavouring to find some *new contrivance* to promote the forementioned things.

3. Resolved, *never to* DO, BE, *or* SUFFER, any thing in soul or body, less or more, but what tends to the glory of God.

---

* These resolutions are extracted from the life of that admirable Christian, and acute reasoner, President J. Edwards. They seem to have had a powerful influence in forming his character. Of the seventy we select the folowing.

4. Resolved, never to lose one moment of *time*, but improve it in the most profitable way I possibly can.

5. Resolved, to live with all my might, while I do live.*

6. Resolved, never to do anything, which I should be afraid to do if it were the last hour of my life.

7. Resolved, to think much, on all occasions, of my own dying, and of the common circumstances which attend death.

8. Resolved, to be endeavoring to find out fit objects of charity and liberality.

9. Resolved, never do anything out of revenge.

---

* This is the full and exact import of the Latin motto "Dum vivimus, vivamus," which was the motto of Dr. Doddridge's family coat-of-arms, and which he has thus paraphrased—

Live, while you live, the EPICURE would say,
And seize the pleasures of the present day;
Live, while you live, the sacred PREACHER cries,
And give to God each moment as it flies.
Lord, in my view let both united be,
I live in PLEASURE when I live to THEE."

10. Resolved, never to suffer the least motion of anger to irrational beings.

11. Resolved, that I will so live as I shall wish I had done when I come to die.

12. Resolved, to live so at all times, as I think it best in my devout frames, and when I have clearest notions of the gospel and another world.

13. Resolved, to maintain strict temperance in eating and drinking.

14. Resolved, never to do anything, which if I should see in another, I should count a just occasion to despise him for, or to think any way the more meanly of him.

15. Resolved, whenever I do any evil action, to trace it back, till I come to the original cause; and then both carefully endeavor to do so no more, and to fight and pray with all my might against the original of it.

16. Resolved, to study the scriptures so steadily, constantly and frequently, as that I may find, and plainly perceive myself to grow in the knowledge of the same.

17. Resolved, to strive to my utmost every week to be brought higher in religion, and to a higher exercise of grace, than I was the week before.

18. Resolved, to be strictly and firmly faithful to my trust, that Prov. xx. 6. *(A faithful man who can find?)* may not be partly fulfilled in me.

19. Resolved, always to do what I can towards making, maintaining, and establishing peace, when it can be done without an overbalancing detriment in other respects.

20. Resolved, never to speak in narrations any thing but the pure and simple truth.

21. Resolved, never to speak evil of any person except some particular good call for it.

22. Resolved, to inquire every night as I am going to bed, wherein I have been negligent, what sin I have committed, and wherein I have denied myself; also at the end of every week, month, and year.

23. Resolved, never to speak anything that is

ridiculous, or matter of laughter on the Lord's day.

24. Resolved, never to do anything that I so much question the lawfulness of, as that I intend, at the same time to consider and examine afterwards, whether it be lawful or no; except I as much question the admission.

25. Resolved, frequently to renew the dedication of myself to God, which was made at my baptism, which I solemnly renewed, when I was received into the communion of the church, and which I have solemnly ratified this 12th day of January, 1723.

26. Resolved, never to act as if I were any way my own, but entirely and altogether God's.

27. Resolved, constantly, with the utmost niceness and diligence, and the strictest scrutiny, to be looking into the state of my soul, that I may know whether I have truly an interest in Christ or no; that when I come to die, I may not have any negligence respecting this to repent of.

28. Resolved, never to give over, nor in the least to slacken my fight with my corruptions, however unsuccessful I may be.

29. Resolved, when I fear misfortunes and adversities, to examine whether I have done my duty, and resolve to do it; and let it be just as Providence orders it, I will as far as I can, be concerned about nothing but my duty, and my sin.

30. Resolved, never to do anything but duty; and then according to Eph. vi. 6—8, do it willingly and cheerfully as unto the Lord, and not to man; knowing that whatever good thing any man doeth, the same shall he receive of the Lord.

31. Resolved, to exercise myself much in this all my life long, viz. with the greatest openness to declare my ways to God, and to lay open my soul to him; all my sins, temptations, difficulties, sorrows, fears, hopes, desires, and everything, and every circumstance, according to Dr. Man-

ton's twenty-seventh sermon on the 119th Psalm.

32. Resolved, after afflictions, to inquire what am I the better for them; what good I *have* got, and what I *might* have got by them.

CONFESSION OF SINS AFTER SELF-EXAMINATION.

O Lord God Almighty, the Judge of all the earth, keeping covenant and mercy to them that love him, and to them that keep his commandments, have mercy upon me a miserable sinner, coming back to thee in the name of Jesus Christ. My conscience accuses me of many transgressions and much disobedience. If in anything I have not greatly sinned, or have in a measure fulfilled thy will, this was the work, and to thee alone be praise. But, O how unfaithful have I been to my engagements, and how often have I transgressed thy law, and been disobedient to thy holy will!

I desire especially to confess and to bewail those sins for which my own heart more particularly condemns me.

And how much of my sinfulness is unknown to myself! But thou art acquainted with all my ways: Oh, cleanse Thou me from my secret faults, and all my known transgressions. Wash me through that precious blood which cleanses from all sin. Give me grace to look to Him who was pierced for my sins, and to mourn for them with that godly sorrow which works repentance unto salvation. Oh, vouchsafe unto me a holy sorrow of heart, a lively faith in Christ, and a sure hope of thy mercy through him, that I may, with a pacified conscience, a believing and penitent, and a grateful and thankful spirit, go to partake of the memorials of his death. Hear me for his name's sake. Amen.

DEVOTIONAL POETRY.

A HYMN OF PRAISE.

[Montgomery.

O God, thou art my God alone,
  Early to thee my soul shall cry,
A pilgrim in a land unknown,
  A thirsty land whose springs are dry.

Oh, that it were as it hath been,
  When, praying in the holy place,
Thy power and glory I have seen,
  And marked the footsteps of thy grace

Yet, through this rough and thorny maze,
  I follow hard on thee, my God;
Thine hand, unseen, upholds my ways,
  I safely tread where thou hast trod.

Thee, in the watches of the night,
Will I remember on my bed;
Thy presence makes the darkness light,
Thy guardian wings are round my head.

Better than life itself thy love,
Dearer than all beside to me;
For whom have I in heaven above,
Or what on earth compared with Thee?

Praise with my heart, my mind, my voice,
Will I for all thy mercies give;
My soul shall still in God rejoice,
My tongue shall bless thee whilst I live.

THE ETERNITY OF GOD.

[Rowe.

Thou didst, O Mighty God, exist
Ere time began its race;
Before the ample elements
Filled up the voids of space:

Before the ponderous earthly globe
In fluid air was stayed;
Before the ocean's mighty springs
Their liquid stores displayed.

Ere men adored, or angels knew,
Or praised thy wondrous name;
Thy bliss, O sacred Spring of life
And glory were the same.

And when the pillars of the world,
With sudden ruin, break;
And all this vast and goodly frame
Sinks in the mighty wreck:

When from her orb the moon shall start,
The astonished sun roll back;
While all the trembling starry lamps
Their ancient course forsake:

Forever permanent and fixed,
From agitation free;
Unchanged, in everlasting years,
Shall thy existence be.

GOD EVERYWHERE.

[Anonymous.

Above—below—where'er I gaze,
Thy guiding finger, Lord, I view,
Traced in the midnight planets' blaze,
Or glistening in the morning dew;
Whate'er is beautiful or fair,
Is but thine own reflection there.

I hear thee in the stormy wind,
That turns the ocean-wave to foam;
Nor less thy wondrous power I find,
When summer airs around me roam;

The tempest and the calm declare
Thyself,—for thou art everywhere.

I find thee in the noon of night,
  And read thy name in every star,
That drinks its splendor from the light
  That flows from mercy's beaming car:
Thy footstool, Lord, each starry gem
Composes—not thy diadem.

And when the radiant orb of light
  Hath tipped the mountain-tops with gold,
Smote with the blaze my weary sight
  Shrinks from the wonders I behold:
That ray of glory bright and fair,
Is but thy living shadow there.

Thine is the silent noon of night,
  The twilight eve—the dewy morn:
Whate'er is beautiful and bright,
  Thine hands have fashioned to adorn;

Thy glory walks in every sphere,
And all things whisper, 'God is here!"

THE BIBLE OUR ONLY TRUE GUIDE.

[Montgomery.

What is the world?—a wildering maze,
Where sin hath tracked ten thousand ways,
Her victims to ensnare;
All broad, and winding, and aslope,
All tempting with perfidious hope,
All ending in despair.

Millions of pilgrims throng these roads,
Bearing their baubles or their loads
Down to eternal night;
One only path that never bends,
Narrow, and rough, and steep, ascends
From darkness into light

Is there no guide to show that path?
The Bible!—He alone who hath
  The Bible need not stray;
But he who hath and will not give
That light of life to all that live,
  Himself shall lose the way.

THE THREE MOUNTAINS.

[Montgomery.

When on Sinai's top I see
God descend in Majesty,
To proclaim his holy law,
All my spirit sinks with awe.

When in ecstacy sublime,
Tabor's glorious height I climb,
In the too transporting light,
Darkness rushes o'er my sight.

When on Calvary I rest,
God in flesh made manifest,
Shines in my Redeemer's face,
Full of beauty, truth, and grace

Here I would for ever stay,
Weep and gaze my soul away;
Thou art heaven on earth to me,
Lovely, mournful Calvary.

FAITH.

[Miss Caroline Fry.

Faith, like an unsuspecting child,
Serenely resting on its mother's arm,
Reposing every care upon her God,
Sleeps on his bosom, and expects no harm.

Receives with joy the promise he makes,
Nor questions of his purpose or his power;

She does not doubting ask, "Can this be so?"
The Lord has said it, and there needs no
more

However deep be the mysterious word,
However dark, she disbelieves it not;
Where Reason would examine, Faith obeys,
And "It is written," answers every doubt.

In vain with rude and overwhelming force
Conscience repeats her tale of misery;
And powers infernal, wakeful to destroy
Urge the worn spirit to despair and die.

As evening's pale and solitary star
But brightens while the darkness gathers
round,
So Faith, unmoved amidst surrounding storms,
Is fairest seen in darkness most profound.

HOPE.

[Cowper.

Hope sets the stamp of vanity on all
That men have deemed substantial since the fall;
Yet has the wondrous virtue to educe
From emptiness itself a real use;
And while she takes, as at a father's hand,
What health and sober appetite demand,
From fading good derives, with chemic art,
That lasting happiness, a thankful heart.
Hope with uplifted foot, set free from earth,
Pants for the place of her etherial birth,
On steady wings sails through th' immense abyss.
Plucks amaranthine joys from bowers of bliss,
And crowns the soul while yet a mourner here,
With wreaths like those triumphant spirits wear.
Hope, as an anchor, firm and sure, holds fast

The Christian vessel, and defies the blast.
Hope! nothing else can nourish or secure
His new-born virtues, and preserve him pure.
Hope! let the wretch, once conscious of the
joy,
Whom now despairing agonies destroy,
Speak, for he can, and none so well as he
What treasures centre, what delights in thee.
Had he the gems, the spices and the land,
That boasts the treasure, all at his command;
The fragrant grove, th' inestimable mine,
Were light, when weighed against one smile
of thine.

THE BELIEVER'S SAFETY.

[Newton.

THAT man no guard nor weapon needs,
Whose heart the blood of Jesus knows;
But safe may pass, if duty leads,
Through burning sand or mountain snows.

Released from guilt, he feels no fear ;
  Redemption is his shield and tower ;
He sees his Saviour always near
  To help in every trying hour.

Though I am weak, and Satan strong,
  And often to assault me tries ;
When Jesus is my shield and song.
  Abashed the wolf before me flies.

His love possessing, I am blest,
  Secure whatever change may come ;
Whither I go, to east or west,
  With him I still shall be at home.

If placed beneath the northern pole,
  Though winter reigns with rigor there ;
His gracious beams would cheer my soul,
  And make a spring throughout the year.

Or if the desert's sun-burnt soil
 My lonely dwelling e'er should prove;
His presence would support my toil,
 Whose smile is life, whose voice is love.

A SOLEMN LITANY.

[Grant.

Saviour! when in dust to thee
Low we bend th' adoring knee,
When repentant to the skies
Scarce we lift our streaming eyes,—
Oh, by all thy pains and wo,
Suffer'd once for man below,
Bending from thy throne on high,
Hear our solemn litany!

By thy helpless infant years—
By thy life of want and tears—

By thy days of sore distress
In the savage wilderness—
By the dread, permitted hour
Of th' insulting Tempter's pow'r—
Turn, O turn, a pitying eye,
Hear our solemn litany!

By the sacred griefs that wept
O'er the grave where Laz'rus slept—
By the boding tears that flow'd
Over Salem's lov'd abode—
By the anguished sigh that told
Treachery lurk'd within thy fold—
From thy seat above the sky,
Hear our solemn litany!

By thine hour of dire despair—
By thine agony of prayer—
By the cross, the nail, the thorn,
Piercing spear, and torturing scorn—

By the gloom that veiled the skies
O'er the dreadful sacrifice—
Listen to our humble cry,
Hear our solemn litany!

By the deep expiring groan—
By the sad sepulchral stone—
By the vault whose dark abode
Held in vain the rising God—
Oh, from earth to heaven restor'd,
Mighty, re-ascended Lord,
Listen, listen to the cry
Of our solemn litany!

VANITY OF LIFE.

[Anon.

What is life?—a rapid stream,
  Rolling onward to the ocean.
What is life?—a troubled dream,
  Full of incident and motion.

What is life ?—the arrow's flight,
  That mocks the keenest gazer's eye.
What is life ?—a gleam of light,
  Darting through a stormy sky.

What is life ?—a varied tale,
  Deeply moving, quickly told.
What is life ?—a vision pale,
  Vanishing while we behold.

What is life ?—a smoke, a vapor,
  Swiftly mingling with the air.
What is life ?—a dying taper,
  The spark that glows to disappear.

What is life ?—a flower that blows.
  Nipped by the frost, and quickly dead.
What is life ?—the full-blown rose,
  That scorched at noon and withered.

Such is life,—a breath, a span,
  A moment quickly gone from thee.
What is death ?—Oh ! mortal man !
  Thy entrance on eternity.

LIFE, DEATH, AND ETERITY.

[Anon.

A SHADOW moving by one's side.
  That would a substance seem,
That is, yet is not,—though descried—
  Like skies beneath the stream :
A tree that's ever in the bloom,
  Whose fruit is never ripe ;
A wish for joys that never come,—
  Such are the hopes of Life.

A dark, inevitable night ;
  A blank that will remain ;
A waiting for the morning light,
  When waiting is in vain ;

A gulf where pathway never led
To show the depth beneath;
A thing we know not, yet we dread,—
That dreaded thing is Death.

The vaulted void of purple sky,
That everywhere extends,
That stretches from the dazzled eye,
In space that never ends;
A morning, whose uprisen sun
No setting e'er shall see;
A day that comes without a noon,—
Such is Eternity.

ON PRAYER.

[Cunningham.

THROUGH the skies when the thunder is
hurl'd
The child to its parent will flee;
Thus amidst the rebukes of the world,
I turn, O my Father, to thee!

In vain would they bid me retire;
In vain would they silence my prayer;
'Tis eye-sight, 'tis life, I require;
I seek to be snatch'd from despair.

In this valley of sorrow and strife,
Prayer shall rise with my earliest breath;
It shall mix in the business of life,
And soften the struggles of death.

ON PRAYER.

Lord, when we bend before thy throne,
  And our confessions pour,
Teach us to feel the sins we own,
  And shun what we deplore.

Our contrite spirits pitying see,
  And penitence impart;
And let a healing ray from thee
  Beam hope upon the heart.

When our responsive tongues essay
  Their grateful songs to raise;
Grant that our souls may join the lay,
  And rise to thee in praise.

When we disclose our wants in prayer
  May we our wills resign;
And not a thought our bosom share,
  Which is not wholly thine.

Let faith each meek petition fill,
  And waft it to the skies;
And teach our hearts 'tis goodness still
  That grants it or denies.

THE COMPLAINT.

[H. K. White.

It is not that my lot is low,
That bids this silent tear to flow;
It is not grief that bids me moan,
It is that I am all alone.

In woods and glens I love to roam,
When the tired hedger hies him home;
Or by the woodland pool to rest,
When pale the star looks on its breast.

Yet when the silent evening sighs
With hallowed air and symphonies,

My spirit takes another tone,
And sighs that it is all alone.

The autumn leaf is sear and dead,
It floats upon the water's bed ;
I would not be a leaf to die,
Without recording sorrow's sigh.

The woods and winds, with sudden wail,
Tell all the same unvaried tale ;
I've none to smile when I am free,
And, when I sigh, to sigh with me.

Yet in my dreams a form I view,
That thinks on me, and loves me too ;
I start, and when the vision's flown,
I weep that I am all alone.

REMONSTRANCE.

[Conder.

But art thou thus indeed alone,
Quite unbefriended—all unknown?
And hast thou then His love forgot,
Who formed thy frame, and fixed thy lot?

Who laid his Son within the grave,
Thy soul from endless death to save:
Who gave his Spirit to console,
And make thy wounded bosom whole?

Is not his voice in evening's gale?
Beams not with him the star so pale?
Is there a leaf can fade or die,
Unnoticed by his watchful eye?

Each fluttering hope, each anxious fear,
Each lonely sigh, each silent tear,
To thine Almighty Friend is known,
And sayest thou, thou art all alone?

FERVENT VOWS AND PETITIONS.

[Moravian Hymn.

THEE will I love, my strength and tower,
 Thee will I love, my joy and crown;
Thee will I love with all my power,
 In all my works, and Thee alone!
Thee will I love, till that pure fire
Fill my whole soul with chaste desire.

In darkness willingly I stray'd;
 I sought Thee, yet from Thee I roved:
For wide my wandering thoughts were spread,
 Thy creatures more than Thee I loved;
And now, if more at length I see,
'Tis through thy light, and comes from Thee.

I thank Thee, uncreated Sun,
 That thy bright beams on me have shin'd
I thank Thee, who hast overthrown
 My foes, and healed my wounde d mind;

I thank Thee, whose enlivening voice
Bids my freed heart in Thee rejoice.

Give to my eyes refreshing tears;
  Give to my heart chaste, hallow'd fires:
Give to my soul, with filial fears,
  The love that all heav'n's host inspires
That all my powers, with all their might,
In thy sole glory may unite.

Thee will I love, my Joy, my Crown!
  Thee will I love, my Lord, my God!
Thee will I love, though all may frown,
  And thorns and briars perplex my road:
Yea, when my flesh and heart decay,
Thee shall I love in endless day.

THE POOR MAN'S PRAYER.

[J. Conder.

As much have I of worldly good
As e'er my master had,
I diet on as dainty food,
And am as richly clad,
Though plain my garb, though scant my board,
As Mary's Son and Nature's Lord.

The manger was his infant bed,
His home the mountain-cave;
He had not where to lay his head,
He borrowed e'en his grave;
Earth yielded him no resting spot,
Her Maker, but she knew him not.

As much the world's good-will I share,
Its favors and applause,
As He whose blessed name I bear,
Hated without a cause;

Despised, rejected, mocked by pride,
Betray'd, forsaken, crucified.

Why should I court my Master's foe?
Why should I fear its frown?
Why should I seek for rest below?
Or sigh for brief renown?
A pilgrim to a better land,
An heir of joy at God's right hand.

HERE AND THERE.

[Hannah More.

HERE, bliss is short, imperfect, insecure;
But total, absolute, and perfect *there.*
Here, time's a moment, short our happiest state;
There, infinite duration is our date.
Here, Satan tempts, and troubles e'en the best;
There Satan's power extends not to the blest;

In a weak simple body, *here* I dwell;
But *there* I drop this frail and sickly shell.
Here, my best thoughts are stained with guilt and fear;
But love and pardon shall be perfect *there*.
Here, my best duties are defiled with sin;
There, all is ease without, and peace within.
Here, feeble faith supplies my only light;
There, faith and hope are swallowed up in sight.
Here, love of self my fairest works destroys,
There, love of God shall perfect all my joys.
Here, things, as in a glass, are darkly shown,
There, I shall know as clearly as I'm known.
Frail are the fairest flowers which bloom below;
There, freshest palms on roots immortal grow.
Here, wants and cares perplex my anxious mind;
But spirits *there* a calm fruition find.

Here, disappointments my best schemes destroy;
There, those that sowed in tears shall reap in joy.
Here, vanity is stamped on all below;
Perfection, *there*, on every good shall grow.
Here, my fond heart is fastened on some friend,
Whose kindness may, whose life must, have an end;
But *there*, no failure can I ever prove,—
God cannot disappoint, for God is love.
Here, Christ for sinners suffered, groaned, and bled;
But *there*, he reigns the great triumphant Head.
Here, mocked and scourged, he wore a crown of thorns;
A crown of glory *there* his brow adorns.

Here, error clouds the will and dims the
sight;
There, all is knowledge, purity and light.
Here, so imperfect is this mortal state,
If blest myself, I mourn some other's fate—
At every human wo I *here* repine;
The joy of every saint shall *there* be mine.
Here, if I lean, the world shall pierce my
heart;
But *there*, that broken reed and I shall part.
Here, on no promised good can I depend;
But *there*, the Rock of ages is my friend.
Here, if some sudden joy delight inspire,
The dread to lose it damps the rising fire;
But *there*, whatever good the soul employ,
The thought, that 'tis eternal, crowns the
joy!

QUESTIONS AND ANSWERS.

[James Montgomery.

FLOWERS, wherefore do ye bloom?
—We strew thy pathway to the tomb.

Stars, wherefore do ye rise?
—To light thy spirit to the skies.

O sun, what makes thy beams so bright?
—The Word that said,—"Let there be light."

Nature, whence sprang thy glorious flame?
—My Maker called me, and I came.

O Light, thy subtle essence who may know?
—Ask not; for all things but myself I show.

What is yon arch which everywhere I see?
—The sign of omnipresent Deity.

Winds, whence and whither do ye blow?
—Thou must be born again to know.

Bow in the cloud, what token dost thou bear;
—That justice still cries "Strike," and mercy "Spare."

Rise, glitter, break; yet, bubble, tell the why?
—To show the course of all beneath the sky.

Ocean, what law thy chainless waves confined?
—That which in reason's limits holds thy mind.

Time, whither dost thou flee?
—I travel to eternity.

Eternity, what art thou,—say?
—Time past, time present, time to come—to-day.

Ye Dead, where can your dwelling be?
—The house for all the living;—come and
see.

O life, what is thy breath?
—A vapor lost in death.

O Death, how ends thy strife?
—In everlasting life.

O Grave, where is thy victory?
—Ask him who rose again for thee.

RETIREMENT.

[Cowper.

FAR from the world, O Lord, I flee,
From strife and danger far;
From scenes where Satan wages still
His most successful war.

The calm retreat, the quiet shade,
  With pray'r and praise agree,
And seem by thy sweet bounty made
  For those who follow thee.

There, if thy Spirit touch the soul,
  And grace her mean abode,
Oh, with what joy, and peace, and love,
  She communes with her God!

There, like the nightingale, she pours
  Her solitary lays,
Nor asks a witness to her song,
  Nor thirsts for human praise.

Author and Guardian of my life,
  Sweet source of light divine!
And, all harmonious names in one,
  My Saviour!—thou art mine!

What thanks I owe thee, and what praise,
A boundless, endless store,
Shall echo through the realms above,
When time shall be no more.

RETIREMENT,

[Cunningham.

Come, escape from the tempests of life,
From the world to the desert retire;
Quit this region of tumult and strife,
To rekindle the heavenly fire.

Poor pilgrim! thy strength must be sought
In the heart-breathing accents of prayer;
In public the battle be fought,
But in secret the weapon prepare.

Oh, rest from thy labors awhile;
Go alone, on the mount, with thy Lord:
Go, bask in the beam of his smile,
And feed on the wealth of his word.

INFLUENCE OF COMMUNION WITH GOD.

[Cowper.

When one, that holds communion with the skies,
Has filled his urn where these pure waters rise,
And once more mingles with us meaner things,
'Tis e'er as if an angel shook his wings;
Immortal fragrance fills the circuit wide,
That tells us whence his treasures are supplied.
So when the ship, well freighted with the stores
The sun matures on India's spicy shores,
Has dropp'd her anchor, and her canvass furl'd,
In some safe haven of our western world,
'Twere vain inquiry to what port she went,
The gale informs us, laden with the scent.

WALKING WITH GOD.

[Cowper.

Oh, for a closer walk with God,
  A calm and heav'nly frame ;
A light to shine upon the road
  That leads me to the Lamb.

Where is the blessedness I knew
  When first I saw the Lord ?
Where is the soul-refreshing view
  Of Jesus and his word ?

What peaceful hours I once enjoy'd !
  How sweet their mem'ry still !
But they have left an aching void,
  The world can never fill.

Return, O holy Dove, return,
  Sweet messenger of rest!
I hate the sins that made thee mourn,
  And drove thee from my breast.

The dearest idol I have known,
Whate'er that idol be;
Help me to tear it from thy throne;
And worship only thee.

So shall my walk be close with God,
Calm and serene my frame:
So purer light shall mark the road
That leads me to the Lamb.

DAILY DUTIES, DEPENDENCE AND ENJOYMENT.

[Christian Observer.

"For whether we live, we live unto the Lord; and whether we die, we die unto the Lord."
Rom. xiv. 9.

When, streaming from the eastern skies,
The morning light salutes my eyes,
O Sun of Righteousness divine,
On me, with beams of mercy, shine;

Chase the dark clouds of guilt away,
And turn my darkness into day.

When to Heaven's great and glorious King,
My morning sacrifice I bring,
And mourning o'er my guilt and shame,
Ask mercy in my Saviour's name,
Then, JESUS, sprinkle with thy blood,
And be my advocate with God.

As every day thy mercy spares,
Will bring its trials and its cares,
O Saviour, till my life shall end,
Be thou my counsellor and friend;
Teach me thy precepts, all divine,
And be thy great example mine.

When pain transfixes every part,
And languor settles at the heart;
When, on my bed, diseased, opprest,
I turn, and sigh, and long for rest;

O great Physician! see my grief,
And grant thy servant sweet relief.

Should Poverty's consuming blow,
Lay all my worldly comforts low,
And neither help nor hope appear,
My steps to guide, my heart to cheer;
Lord! pity and supply my need,
For thou on earth, wast poor indeed.

Should Providence profusely pour
Its various blessings in my store,
O keep me from the ills, that wait
On such a seeming prosperous state:
From hurtful passions set me free,
And humbly may I walk with thee.

When each day's scenes and labors close,
And wearied nature seeks repose,
With pardoning mercy richly blest,
Guard me, my Saviour, while I rest:

And, as each morning sun shall rise,
O lead me onward to the skies.

And, at my life's last setting sun,
My conflicts o'er, my labors done;
Jesus, thine heavenly radiance shed,
To cheer and bless my dying bed.
And from death's gloom my spirit raise,
"To see thy face, and sing thy praise."

THE BIRTH OF CHRIST.

[Heber.

BRIGHTEST and best of the sons of the morning,
Dawn on our darkness, and lend us thine aid!
Star of the east the horizon adorning,
Guide where our infant Redeemer is laid.

Cold on his cradle the dew-drops are shining,
Low lies his bed with the beasts of the stall;
Angels adore him in slumber reclining,
Maker, and Monarch, and Saviour of all.

Say, shall we yield him, in costly devotion,
Odors of Eden, and offerings divine,
Gems of the mountain, and pearls of the ocean,
Myrrh from the forest, and gold from the mine?

Vainly we offer each ample oblation;
Vainly with gold would his favor secure;
Richer by far is the heart's adoration,
Dearer to God are the prayers of the poor!

Brightest and best of the sons of the morning,
Dawn on our darkness, and lend us thine aid!
Star of the east the horizon adorning,
Guide where our infant Redeemer is laid.

LIVING TO CHRIST.

[Moravian Hymn.

O draw me, Saviour, after Thee,
So shall I run and never tire
With gracious words still comfort me:
Be Thou, my hope, my sole desire
Free me from every weight: nor fear
Nor sin can come, if Thou art here.

In suffering be thy love my peace,
  In weakness be thy love my power:
And when the storms of life shall cease
  Jesus, in that important hour,
In death, as life, be thou my guide,
And save me, who for me hast died!

FORSAKING ALL FOR CHRIST.

[Grant.

Jesus, I my cross have taken,
  All to leave, and follow thee;
Naked, poor, despis'd, forsaken,
  Thou, from hence, my all shall be;
Perish every fond ambition,
  All I've sought, or hop'd, or known,
Yet how rich is my condition,
  God and heaven are still my own.

Let the world despise and leave me;
  They have left my Saviour too:
Human hearts and looks deceive me,
  Thou art not, like them, untrue;
And whilst thou shalt smile upon me,
  God of wisdom, love, and might,
Foes may hate, and friends may scorn me,
  Show thy face, and all is bright.

Go, then, earthly fame and treasure,
  Come disaster, scorn, and pain,
In thy service pain is pleasure,
  With thy favor loss is gain.
I have call'd thee Abba, Father,
  I have set my heart on thee,
Storms may howl, and clouds may gather,
All must work for good to me.

Man may trouble and distress me,
  'Twill but drive me to thy breast;

Life with trials hard may press me,
  Heaven will bring me sweeter rest.
Oh! 'tis not in grief to harm me,
  While thy love is left to me;
Oh! 'twere not in joy to charm me;
  Were that joy unmix'd with thee.

Soul, then know thy full salvation,
  Rise o'er sin, and fear, and care,
Joy to find in every station
  Something still to do or bear;
Think what Spirit dwells within thee;
  Think what Father's smiles are thine;
Think that Jesus died to win thee:
  Child of heaven canst thou repine?

Haste thee on from grace to glory,
  Arm'd by faith, and wing'd by prayer;
Heaven's eternal days before thee,
  God's own hand shall guide thee there.

Soon shall close thy earthly mission,
Soon shall pass thy pilgrim days;
Hope shall change to glad fruition,
Faith to sight, and prayer to praise.

MEDITATING ON THE CROSS.

SWEET the moments, rich in blessing
Which before the cross I spend;
Life, and health, and peace possessing
From the sinner's dying Friend.
Here I'll sit for ever viewing,
Mercy's streams in streams of blood
Precious drops my soul bedewing,
Plead and calm my peace with God.

Truly blessed is this station,
Low before his cross to lie,
While I see divine compassion
Floating in his languid eye:

Here it is I find my heaven,
While upon the Lamb I gaze,
Love I much?—I've much forgotten,
I'm a miracle of grace.

Love and grief my heart dividing,
With my tears his feet I'll bathe,
Constant still in faith abiding,
Life deriving from his death:
May I still enjoy this feeling,
In all need to Jesus go;
Prove his wounds each day more healing,
And himself more deeply know.

A SACRAMENTAL HYMN.

Bread of heaven!—on thee I feed,
For thy flesh is meat indeed;
Ever may my soul be fed
With this true and living bread;

Day by day with strength supplied,
Through the life of him who died.

Vine of heaven!—thy blood supplies
This blest cup of sacrifice.
'Tis thy wounds my healing give:
To thy cross I look, and live.
Thou, my life! Oh! let me be
Rooted, grafted, built on thee!

THIS DO IN REMEMBRANCE OF ME.

[Noel.

If human kindness meets return,
  And owns the grateful tie;
If tender thoughts within us burn,
  To feel a friend is nigh:

Oh, shall not warmer accents tell
The gratitude we owe
To Him who died, our fears to quell,
Our more than orphan's wo !

While yet his anguish'd soul survey'd
Whose pangs he would not flee ;
What love his latest words display'd—
" Meet and remember me !"

Remember Thee !—thy death, thy shame,
Our sinful hearts to share :
Oh, memory, leave no other name
But His recorded there !

COMFORT IN AFFLICTION.

[Moore.

Oh, thou who dry'st the mourner's tear,
How dark this world would be,
If, when deceiv'd and wounded here,
We could not fly to thee !

The friends who in our sunshine live,
When winter comes, are flown;
And he who has but tears to give,
Must weep those tears alone;
But thou wilt heal that broken heart,
Which, like the plants that throw
Their fragrance from the wounded part,
Breathes sweetness out of wo.

When joy no longer soothes or cheers,
And e'en the hope that threw
A moment's sparkle o'er our tears,
Is dimm'd and vanish'd too!
Oh, who could bear life's stormy doom,
Did not thy wing of love
Come brightly wafting through the gloom
One Peace-Branch from above!
Then sorrow, touched by thee, grows bright
With more than rapture's ray;
As darkness shows us worlds of light
We never saw by day.

COMFORT UNDER AFFLICTION.

[Grant.

When gathering clouds around I view,
And days are dark, and friends are few,
On Him I lean, who not in vain
Experienced every human pain.
He sees my griefs, allays my fears,
And counts and treasures up my tears.

If aught should tempt my soul to stray
From heavenly wisdom's narrow way;
To fly the good I would pursue,
Or do the thing I would not do;
Still He, who felt temptation's power,
Shall guard me in that dangerous hour.

If wounded love my bosom swell,
Despised by those I prized too well;
He shall his pitying aid bestow,
Who felt on earth severer wo;

At once betrayed, denied, or fled,
By those who shared his daily bread.

When vexing thoughts within me rise,
And, sore dismayed, my spirit dies;
Yet He who did vouchsafe to bear
The sickening anguish of despair,
Shall sweetly soothe, shall gently dry,
The throbbing heart, the streaming eye.

When mourning o'er some stone I bend,
Which covers all that was a friend;
And from his voice, his hand, his smile,
Divides me for a little while;
Thou, Saviour, mark'st the tears I shed,
For thou didst weep o'er Lazarus dead.

And O! when I have safely passed
Through every conflict but the last;
Still, still unchanging, watch beside
My painful bed—for thou hast died;

Then point to realms of cloudless day,
And wipe the latest tear away.

RESIGNATION.

[Edmeston.

Oh, thou whose mercy guides my way,
Though now it seem severe;
Forbid my unbelief to say,
There is no mercy here!

Oh, grant me to desire the pain
That comes in kindness down,
More than the world's supremest gain
Succeeded by a frown.

Then, though thou bend my spirit low,
Love only shall I see;
The very hand that strikes the blow
Was wounded once for me.

RESIGNATION TO PROVIDENCE.

[Darwin.

THE Lord; how tender is his love,
His justice, how august;
Hence all her fears my soul derives,
There anchors all her trust.

He showers the manna from above,
To feed the barren waste;
Or points with death the rushing hail,
And famine waits the blast.

He bids distress forget to groan,
The sick from anguish cease;
In dungeons spreads his healing wing,
And softly whispers—*peace.*

His vengeance rides the rushing wind
Or tips the bolt with flame:
His goodness breathes in every breeze,
And warms in every beam.

For me, O Lord! whatever lot
  The hours commissioned bring;
If all my withering blessings die,
  Or fairer clusters spring;

Oh! grant that still with grateful heart,
  My years resigned may run;
'Tis thine to give, or to resume;
  And may thy will be done!

THE COVENANTERS' COMMUNION.

[Vedder.

WHEN the orb of morn enlightens
  Hill and mountain, mead and dell;
When the dim horizon brightens,
  And the serried clouds dispel;
And the sun-flower eastward bending,
  Its fidelity to prove:—
Be thy gratitude ascending
  Unto him whose name is Love.

When the vesper-star is beaming
  In the coronet of even;
And the lake and river gleaming
  With the ruddy hues of heaven;
When a thousand notes are blending
  In the forest and the grove;—
Be thy gratitude ascending
  Unto him whose name is Love.

When the stars appear in millions,
  In the portals of the west,
Bespangling the pavilions
  Where the blessed are at rest;
When the milky-way is glowing
  In the cope of heaven above;—
Let thy gratitude be flowing
  Unto him whose name is Love.

COMMUNION WITH CHRIST.

[Noel.

WHEN in the hours of lonely wo,
I give my sorrows leave to flow;
And anxious fear and dark distrust
Weigh down my spirit to the dust:

When not e'en friendship's gentle aid
Can heal the wounds the world has made,
Oh, this shall check each rising sigh,—
That Jesus is forever nigh.

His counsels and upholding care
My safety and my comfort are;
And he shall guide me all my days,
Till glory crown the work of grace.

Jesus, in whom but thee above
Can I repose my trust, my love?

And shall an earthy object be
Lov'd in comparison with thee?

My flesh is hastening to decay,
Soon shall the world have pass'd away;
And what can mortal friends avail,
When heart, and strength, and life shall fail?

But oh, be thou my Saviour nigh,
And I will triumph while I die!
My strength, my portion is divine,
And Jesus is for ever mine!

SEPARATION.

[Anon.

When forced to part from those we love,
If sure to meet to-morrow,
We still a pang of anguish prove,
And feel a touch of sorrow.

But who can paint the briny tears
  We shed when thus we sever,
If forced to part, for months, for years,
  To part—perhaps *for ever!*

ANSWER

[Dudley.

But if our thoughts are fixed aright,
  A cheering hope is given,
Though *here* our prospects end in night,
  We meet again in heaven.

Yes, if our souls are raised above,
  'Tis sweet when thus we sever,
Since parting in a Saviour's love,
  We part *to meet for ever!*

WHAT IS LIFE?

[H. G. R.

I ASKED a man of sorrow and of tears,
Whose looks told anguish pressed him more
than years;
He mused awhile, and then distinctly said,
"Life is burden—would that I were dead."

I asked a Christian who had early strayed
From virtue's paths; this was the answer
made—
"Life is a precious boon to mortals given,
Which, if well spent, will be renewed in
heaven."

I asked a youth, whose cheerfulness of mien
Bespoke him happy in this active scene;
He told me 'twas "a poet's golden dream;"
And leaving me, rushed forward with the
stream.

I questioned age; it heaved a heavy sigh,
Expressing volumes; this was its reply—
"Life is at best but a tempestuous sea,
That fast rolls onward to eternity."

I asked myself, a voice appeared to say—
"Beware you value it while yet you may;
'Tis a rich gift thy God bestowed on thee;
Abuse it not—'twere better not to be."

WHAT IS TIME?

[Marsden.

I ASKED an aged man, a man of cares,
Wrinkled, and curved, and white with hoary
hairs;
"Time is the *warp* of life," he said, "O tell
The young, the fair, the gay to weave it
well!"

I asked the ancient venerable dead,
Sages who wrote, and warriors who bled;
From the cold grave a hollow murmur flowed,
"Time sowed the *seeds* we reap in this abode!"

I asked a dying sinner, ere the stroke
Of ruthless death life's "golden bowl had broke;"
I asked him, What is time? "Time," he replied,
"I've lost it. Ah the *treasure!*" and he died!

I asked the golden sun and silver spheres,
Those bright chronometers of days and years;
They answered, "Time is but a *meteor's* glare,"
And bade me for eternity prepare.

I asked the seasons, in their annual round
Which beautify, or desolate the ground;
And they replied, (no oracle more wise,)
"'Tis folly's *blank*, and wisdom's highest *prize!*"

I asked a spirit lost, but, O the shriek
That pierced my soul! I shudder while I speak!
It cried, "A *particle!* a *speck!* a mite
Of endless years, duration infinite!"

Of things inanimate, my dial I
Consulted, and it made me this reply,
"Time is the season fair of living well,
The path to glory, or the path to hell."

I asked my Bible, and methinks it said,
"Thine is the present hour the past is fled;
Live! live to-day! *to-morrow* never yet,
On any human being, rose or set!"

I asked old father Time himself at last;
But in a moment he flew swiftly past;
His chariot was a cloud, the viewless wind
His noisless steeds, that left no trace behind.

I asked the mighty angel, who shall stand,
One foot on sea, and one on solid land:
"By heaven's great King, I swear the mystery's o'er!
Time *was*," he cried,—"but time shall be no more!"

TO-MORROW. Proverbs xxvii. 2.

[Knox.

To-MORROW!—mortal, boast not thou
Of time and tide that are not now!
But think, in one revolving day
How earthly things may pass away!

To-day—while hearts with rapture spring,
The youth to beauty's lip may cling;
To-morrow—and that lip of bliss
May sleep unconscious of his kiss.

To-day—the blooming spouse may press
Her husband in a fond caress;
To-morrow—and the hands that pressed
May wildly strike her widowed breast.

To-day—the clasping babe may drain
The milk-stream from its mother's vein;
To-morrow, like a frozen rill,
That bosom-current may be still.

To-day—thy merry heart may feast
On herb and fruit, and bird and beast;
To-morrow—spite of all thy glee,
The hungry worms may feast on thee.

To-morrow !—mortal, boast not thou
Of time and tide that are not now !
But think, in one revolving day
That e'en thyself may'st pass away.

HOPE IN THE RESURRECTION.

[H. K. White.

THROUGH sorrow's night, and danger's path,
Amid the deepening gloom,
We soldiers of an injured King
Are marching to the tomb.

There, when the turmoil is no more,
And all our powers decay,
Our cold remains in solitude
Shall sleep the years away.

Our labors done, securely laid
  In this our last retreat,
Unheeded o'er our silent dust
  The storms of life shall beat.

Yet not thus lifeless, thus inane,
  The vital spark shall lie,
For o'er life's wreck that spark shall rise,
  To seek its kindred sky.

These ashes too, this little dust,
  Our Father's care shall keep,
Till the last angel rise and break
  The long and dreary sleep.

Then love's soft dew o'er every eye,
  Shall shed its mildest rays,
And the long silent dust shall burst
  With shouts of endless praise.

RESURRECTION.

[Anon.

Our life how short ! a groan, a sigh ;
We live—and then begin to die :
But oh ! how great a mercy this,
That death's a portal into bliss !

My soul ! death swallows up thy fears
My grave-clothes wi way all tears ;
Why should we fear this parting pain,
Who die, that we may live again.

STEADY PURSUIT OF HEAVEN.

[Moore.

The dove let loose in eastern skies,
  Returning fondly home,
Ne'er stoops to earth her wing, nor flies
  Where idler warblers roam ;

But high she shoots through air and light,
Above all low delay.
Where nothing earthly bounds her flight,
Nor shadow dims her way.

So grant me, Lord ! from every stain,
Of sinful passion free,
Aloft, through virtue's purer air,
To steer my course to thee !

No sin to cloud, no lure to stay,
My soul, as home she springs,
Thy sunshine on her joyful way,
Thy freedom on her wings.

HEAVEN.

[Bowring.

THE golden palace of my God
  Towering above the clouds I see,
Beyond the cherub's bright abode,
  Higher than angels' thoughts can be:
How can I in those courts appear,
  Without a wedding-garment on?
Conduct me, thou life-giver, there,
  Conduct me to thy glorious throne;
And clothe me with thy robes of light,
And lead me through sin's darksome night,
    My Saviour and my God.

THE HEAVENLY REST.

[Anon.

THERE is an hour of peaceful rest,
  To mourning wanderers given;

There is a joy for souls distressed,
A balm for every wounded breast—
'Tis found above—in heaven.

There is a soft, a downy bed,
'Tis fair as breath of even,
A couch for weary mortals spread,
Where they may rest the aching head,
And find repose, in heaven!

There is a home for weary souls,
By sin and sorrow driven;
When tossed on life's tempestuous shoals,
Where storms arise, and ocean rolls,
And all is drear but heaven!

There faith lifts up her cheerful eye
To brighter prospects given;
And views the tempest passing by,
The evening shadows quickly fly
And all serene in heaven!

There fragrant flowers, immortal bloom,
And joys supreme are given:
There rays divine disperse the gloom:
Beyond the confines of the tomb,
Appears the dawn of heaven.

THE HEAVENLY SABBATH.

[Doddridge.

Lord of the Sabbath, hear our vows,
On this thy day, in this thine house;
And own, as grateful sacrifice,
The songs which from the desert rise.

Thine earthly Sabbaths, Lord, we love;
But there's a nobler rest above;
To that our laboring souls aspire,
With ardent hope and strong desire.

No more fatigue, no more distress,
Nor sin, nor death, shall reach that place ;
No tears shall mingle with the songs
That warble from immortal tongues.

No rude alarms of raging foes,
No cares to break the long repose,
No midnight shade, no clouded sun—
But sacred, high, eternal noon.

O long expected day, begin ;
Dawn on these realms of wo and sin
Fain would we leave this weary road
And sleep in death to rest with God.

THE HEAVENLY TEMPLE.

[Logan.

WHERE high the heavenly temple stands,
The house of God not made with hands,

A great High Priest our nature wears,
The guardian of mankind appears.

He who for men their surety stood,
And pour'd on earth his precious blood,
Pursues in heaven his mighty plan,
The Saviour and the friend of man.

Though now ascended up on high,
He bends on earth a brother's eye ;
Partaker of the human name,
He knows the frailty of our frame.

Our fellow-suff 'rer yet retains
A fellow-feeling of our pains,
And still remembers in the skies,
His tears, his agonies, and cries.

In every pang that rends the heart,
The Man of sorrows had a part ;

He sympathizes with our grief,
And to the suff'rer sends relief

With boldness, therefore, at the throne
Let us make all our sorrows known,
And ask the aids of heavenly power,
To help us in the evil hour.

THE DAY AFTER JUDGMENT.

[Montgomery.

THE days and years of time are fled,
Sun, moon, and stars have shone their last,
The earth and sea gave up their dead,
Then vanished at the archangel's blast:
All secret things have been revealed,
Judgment is past, the sentence sealed,
And man to all eternity
What he is *now* henceforth must be,

From Adam to his youngest heir,
  Not one escaped that muster-roll;
Each, as if he alone were there,
  Stood up, and won or lost his soul;
These from the Judge's presence go
Down into everlasting wo;
Vengeance hath barred the gates of hell,
The scenes within no tongue can tell.

But lo! far off the righteous pass
  To glory from the King's right hand;
In silence, on the sea of glass,
  Heaven's numbers without number stand,
While he who bore the cross lays down
His priestly robe and victor-crown;
The mediatorial reign complete,
All things are put beneath his feet.

Then every eye in Him shall see,
  (While thrones and powers before him
    fall,)

The fulness of the Deity.
  Where God himself is all in all:
O how eternity shall ring
While the first note the ransomed sing!
While in that strain all voices blend,
Which once begun shall never end.

In that unutterable song,
  Shall I employ immortal breath?
Or with the wicked borne along,
  For ever die, the "second death?"
Jesus, my life, my light thou art;
Thy word is in my mouth, my heart;
Lord, I believe,—my spirit save
From sinking lower than the grave.

ON TIME.

[Selleck Osborne.

MOVED by a strange mysterious power,
That hastes along the rapid hour,

I touch the deep-toned string;
Even now I saw his withered face
Beneath yon tower's mouldering base,
Where mossy vestments cling.

Dark rolled his cheerless eye around,
Severe his grisly visage frowned,
No locks his head arrayed;
He grasped a hero's antique bust;
The marble crumbled into dust,
And sunk amidst the shade!

Malignant triumph filled his eyes;
"See, hapless mortals, see," he cries,
"How vain your idle schemes.
Beneath my grasp, the fairest form
Dissolves and mingles with the worm;
Thus vanish mortal dreams.

"The works of God and man I spoil;
The noblest proof of human toil

I treat as childish toys—
I crush the noble and the brave;
Beauty I mar, and in the grave
I bury human joys."

'Hold! ruthless phantom, hold!' I cried;
If thou canst mock the dreams of pride,
And meaner hopes devour—
Virtue, beyond thy reach shall bloom,
When other charms sink to the tomb.
She scorns thy envious power.

On frosty wings the demon fled,
Howling, as o'er the wall he sped,
"Another year is gone!"
The ruined spire—the crumbling tower,
Nodding obeyed his awful power,
As TIME flew swiftly on.

Since beauty then to time must bow,
And age deform the fairest brow,

Let brighter charms be yours—
The female mind, embalmed in truth,
Shall bloom in everlasting youth,
While Time himself endures.

FALLS OF NIAGARA.*

[Robert Fletcher.

Beyond the deep Atlantic waves,
These fair but faded flowerets grew;
Where dread Niagara falls and raves,
They sipped the pearls of morning dew;
The parent root that gave them birth,
Still beautifies the distant earth!

* Note.—In May 1828, when the Rev. Wm. Patton, of New York, was on a visit to the Rev. Joseph Fletcher, of Stepney, London, having occasion to refer to his Pocket-Testament, in which he found deposited several small wild flowers, which he had plucked at the Falls of Niagara on the preceding summer, the conversation turned upon that stupendous waterfall. Robert, the eldest son, who had listened with deep interest to the description which was given now left the room, and in about thirty minutes returned, with the accompanying stanzas.

'Tis Spring! and many a lovely flower,
Clustering around that root appears,
Each nurtured by a gentle shower
Of the deep torrent's rainbow tears;
And each rewarding the wild bee
With nectar for his minstrelsy.

Sweet flowers! How glorious was your home!
Where, startling *earth's* deep caves with fright,
And shaking *heaven's* eternal dome,
Gigantic cataracts day and night,
Adown the steep, with thundering whirl,
Their endless lightning waters hurl!

Built by the golden sun by day,
And by the silvery moon by night,
Is seen, amidst the torrent's spray,
An everlasting rainbow's light;
Serene above the cataract's rage,
Cheering the storm it can't assuage!

But while her hues these flowers recall,
With all the wonders of their clime,
Mortal! hear'st thou not the "fall"
Of the dark rolling stream of "time"
Into a deep eternity?
Is mercy's bow there spread for thee?

SONG OF A CHILD ON HEARING THE WIND BLOW.

The leading ideas of the following lines were really entertained by a young lady when a child.

I love to listen when winds blow high,
And hear the music of the sky,
Because, I think 'tis the angel's song,
That sounds when the fleet wind sweeps along.
Swift as they ride on the cars of cloud,
Hark, how they sing to their fellows aloud!

We catch not the words, but the sweet notes
swell
Down here; and this music I love so well,
Sounds like the distant notes of the lay,
Borne by the gentle breeze away,
When the earthly good, from their humble
abode,
Send up their evening praise to God.

Now with awe their voices are still,
Now there's a sound so sweet and shrill,
It must be an infant such as I,
But lately a tenant of the sky,
Trying the powers of his little voice,
While the rest all listen—now, now they re-
joice,
And join with him in the praise of God,
Who washed his young spirit in Jesus'
blood,
And took him away from mortal sorrow,

Before his little heart was riven,
For a bright long day without a morrow,
To unite with them in the songs of heaven.

I wish, that his mother, who weeps for him,
Could hear the sound of his joyful hymn,
And see how happy her child is there
In those blue regions, so soft and fair;
I'm sure she'd never weep again,
If she could hear that heavenly strain.

Mother! if I should ever go,
Where the angels are sitting so,
I'll sing so loud, that the winds shall bear
My voice on their wings to my mother's ear;
And I'll tell you not to weep for me,
For Mary is happy as she can be;
And I'll pray the Highest to send for you,
And when you have done what He's given
you to do,

Oh then, my mother, you shall come,
Happy and glad to your daughter's home.

THERE IS A WORLD WE HAVE NOT SEEN.

[Anon.

There is a world we have not seen,
  Which time shall never dare destroy,
Where mortal footstep hath not been,
  Nor ear hath caught its sounds of joy.

There is a region lovelier far
  Than sages tell, or poets sing,
Brighter than summer beauties are,
  And softer than the tints of spring.

It is all holy and serene,
  The land of glory and repose;
And there, to dim the radiant scene,
  The tear of sorrow never flows.

It is not fanned by summer gale,
'Tis not refreshed by summer showers,
It never needs the moon-beam pale,
For there are known no evening hours.

In vain the philosophic eye
May seek to view the fair abode,
Or find it in the curtained sky—
It is the dwelling-place of God!

RETIREMENT.

[Bowring.

" He was there alone" when even
Had round earth its mantle thrown;
Holding intercouse with heaven,
" He was there alone."

There his inmost heart's emotion
Made he to his Father known;
In the spirit of devotion.
Musing there "alone."

So let us, from earth retiring,
Seek our God and Father's throne;
And to other scenes aspiring,
"Train our hearts alone."

Thus when time its course hath ended,
And the joys of earth are flown,
We, by hope and bliss attended,
Shall not be "alone."

Bickersteth's Treatise on Prayer. 18mo. 40
Treatise on the Lord's Supper. 18mo. 30
Blunt's Undesigned Coincidences in the Writings both of the Old and New Testaments, an Argument of their Veracity. 8vo. 1 25
Bogatzky's Golden Treasury. 18mo. 50
Bonar's Night of Weeping. 18mo. 30
Story of Grace. 18mo. 30
Bonnet's Family of Bethany. 18mo. 40
Meditations on the Lord's Prayer. 18mo. 40
Borrow's Bible and Gypsies of Spain. 8vo. cloth 75
Boston's Four-fold State. 18mo. 50
Crook in the Lot. 18mo. 30
Brown's Explication of the Assembly's Catechism. 12mo. 60
Bridges On the Christian Ministry. 8vo. 1 50
On the Proverbs. 8vo. 2 00
On the cxix Psalm. 12mo. 75
Memoir of Mary Jane Graham.
Works. 3 vols. 8vo.
Buchanan's Comfort in Affliction. 18mo. 40
On the Holy Spirit, 12mo. 1 00
Bunbury's Glory, Glory, Glory, and other Narratives. 18mo. 25
Butler's Complete Works. 8vo. 1 50
Sermons, alone. 8vo. 1 00
Analogy, alone. 8vo. 75
and Wilson's Analogy. 8vo. 1 25
Bunyan's Jerusalem Sinner Saved. 18mo 50
Greatness of the Soul. 18mo. 50
Burns' Christian Fragments. 18mo. 40
Calvin on Secret Providence 18mo. 25
Cameron's Farmer's Daughter. 18mo. 30
Catechisms—The Assembly's Catechism. per hundred 1 25
Do. with Proofs 3 00
Brown's Short Catechism. Per hundred 1 25
Smyth's Ecclesiastical Catechism. 18mo 25
Key to the Assembly's Catechism. 18mo. 20

Catechism. Willison's Communicant's. 18mo.	10
Cecil's Works; comprising his Sermons, Miscellanies, and Remains. 3 vols. 12mo.	2 00
Remains, separate	60
Original Thoughts on Scripture; being the Substance of Sermons, taken down by Mrs. Hawkes, and now edited by Catherine Cecil.	
Charnock's Choice Works. 12mo.	6
Chalmers' Select Works; comprising his Miscellanies, Lectures on Romans, and Sermons. 4 vols. 8vo.	6 00
Romans, separate	1 50
Miscellanies, "	1 50
Sermons. 2 vols. separate	2 50
Evidences of Christian Revelation. 2 vols.	1 25
Natural Theology. 2 vols.	1 25
Moral Philosophy	60
Commercial Discourses	60
Astronomical Discourses	60
Christian Retirement. 12mo.	75
Experience. By the same Author. 18mo.	50
Clark's Walk About Zion, 12mo.	75
Pastor's Testimony	75
Awake, Thou Sleeper	75
Young Disciple	88
Gathered Fragments	1 00
Clarke's Daily Scripture Promises. 32mo. gilt	30
Colquhoun's World's Religion. 18mo.	30
Cunningham's World Without Souls. 18mo.	30
Cummings' Message from God, 18mo.	30
David's Psalms, in metre. Large type and fine paper, most elegant edition. 12mo. embossed	75
Do Do Turkey mor.	2 00
Do. 18mo. good type, plain sheep	38
Do. 48mo. very neat pocket edition. mor.	25
Do. " " gilt edge	31
Do. " " tucks	50

Davies' Sermons. 3 vols. 12mo.	2 00
Davidson's Connexions. 3 vols 12mo.	1 50
Davis' Boatman's Manual. 18mo.	30
Sailor's Companion. 18mo.	30
D'Aubigne's History of the Reformation. *Carefully revised,* with various additions not hitherto published. 4 vols. 12mo. half cloth	1 50
Do. " " full cloth	1 75
Do. " " 4th vol. half cloth	38
Do. " " " full cloth	50
Do. Complete in one volume	1 00
Life of Cromwell. 12mo.	50
Germany, England, and Scotland. 12mo.	75
Luther and Calvin. 18mo.	25
Dick's Lectures on Acts. 8vo.	1 50
Doddridge's Rise and Progress. 18mo.	40
Life of Colonel Gardiner. 18mo.	30
Duncan's (Rev. Henry) Sacred Philosophy of the Seasons. 4 vols. 12mo.	3 00
Tales of the Scottish Peasantry. 18mo.	50
Cottage Fireside. 18mo.	40
Life. By his Son. With portrait. 12mo.	75
(Mrs.) Life of Mary Lundie Duncan. 18mo.	50
Life of George A. Lundie. 18mo.	50
Memoir of George B. Philips. 18mo.	25
Erskine's Gospel Sonnets. New and beautiful edition.	
Ferguson's Roman Republic. 8vo.	
Fisk's Memorial of the Holy Land. With steel plates	1 00
Fleury's Life of David. 12mo.	60
Foster's Essays, on Decision of Character, &c., large type, fine edition. 12mo.	75
close type. 18mo.	50
Ford's Decapolis. 18mo.	25
Free Church Pulpit: consisting of Discourses by the most eminent Divines of the Free Church of Scotland. 3 vols. 8vo.	5 00

Fry (Caroline) The Listener. 2 vols in one	1 00
Christ our Law. 12mo.	60
Sabbath Musings. 18mo.	40
The Scripture Reader's Guide. 18mo.	30
Geological Cosmogony. By a Layman. 18mo.	30
God in the Storm. 18mo.	25
Griffith's Live while you Live. 18mo.	30
Graham's (Mrs. Isabella), Life and Writings. 12mo.	60
(Miss Mary J), Life and Works. 8vo.	
Test of Truth. Separate. 18mo.	30
Haldane's Exposition of Romans. 8vo.	2 50
Hamilton's Life in Earnest—Mount of Olives—Harp on the Willows—Thankfulness—and Life of Bishop Hall, each	30
Hawker's Poor Man's Morning Portion. 12mo.	60
" Evening Portion. "	60
Zion's Pilgrim. 18mo.	30
Hervey's Meditations "	40
Hetherington's History of the Church of Scotland from the introduction of Christianity to the period of the disruption in 1843. Fifth edition	1 50
Henry's Method for Prayer	40
Communicant's Companion. 18mo.	40
Daily Communion with God. "	30
Pleasantness of a Religious Life. "	30
Choice Works. 12mo.	60
Hills (George) Lectures on Divinity. 8vo.	2 00
(Rowland) Life. By Sidney. 12mo.	75
History of the Reformation in Europe. 18mo.	40
Housman's Life and Remains. 12mo.	75
Horne's (Thos. H.) Introduction to the Study of the Bible. 2 vols. royal 8vo. Half cloth.	3 50
Do do. 1 vol., sheep.	4 00
Do, do. 2 vols., cloth.	4 00
(Bishop) Commentary on the Book of Psalms. With Irving's Introd. Essay. 8vo.	1 50

Howell's Life.—Perfect Peace. 18mo.	30
Howe's Redeemer's Tears and other Essays. 18mo.	50
Huss' (Jno.) Life. Translated from the German.	25
Jacobus on Matthew. With a Harmony. **Illustrated.**	75
James' Anxious Enquirer. 18mo.	30
True Christian. "	30
Widow Directed. "	30
Janeway's Heaven upon Earth. 12mo.	60
Token for Children. 18mo.	30
Jay's Morning Exercises. 12mo.	75
Evening " "	75
Christian Contemplated. 18mo.	40
Jubilee Memorial. "	30
Jerram's Tribute to a beloved and only Daughter.	30
Key to the Shorter Catechism. 18mo.	20
Kennedy's (Grace) Profession is not Principle. 18mo.	30
Jessy Allan, the Lame Girl. 18mo.	25
Krummacher's Martyr Lamb. 18mo.	40
Elijah, the Tishbite. "	40
Last Days of Elisha 12mo.	75
Life in New York. 18mo.	40
Lowrie's Letters to Sabbath School Children. 18mo.	25
Lockwood's Memoir. By his Father. 18mo.	40
Luther's Commentary on Galatians. 8vo.	1 50
Mackay—The Wycliffites; or England in 15th Century.	75
Martin's (Sarah) Life. 18mo.	30
Martyn's (Henry) Life. 12mo.	60
Mason's Essays on the Church. 12mo.	60
" on Episcopacy. "	60
Martyrs and Covenanters of Scotland. 18mo.	40
Malcom on the Atonement. 18mo.	30
McCrindell—The Convent, a Narrative. 18mo.	50
McGilvray's Peace in Believing. 18mo.	25
McCheyne's (Rev. Robert Murray) Works, comprising his Life, Lectures, Letters, and Sermons. To which is now added the "Familiar Letters." 2 vols., 8vo.	3 00

McCheynes Life, Lectures, and Letters. Separate. To which is also added his "Familiar Letters."	1 50
Sermons. Separate.	2 00
Familiar Letters from the Holy Land. 18mo,	50
McLeod's Life and Power of True Godliness. 12mo.	60
Meikle's Solitude Sweetened. 12mo.	60
Miller's (Rev. Dr. Samuel) Memoir of Rev. Dr. Nisbet.	75
(Rev. John) Design of the Church. 12mo.	60
Michael Kemp, the Farmer's Lad. 18mo.	40
Monod's Lucilla; or the Reading of the Bible. 18mo.	40
Missions, the Origin and History of. By Choules and Smith. With 25 steel plates. Quarto.	3 50
Morell's Historical and Critical View of the Speculative Philosophy of Europe in the 19th Century	3 00
My School Boy Days. 18mo.	30
My Youthful Companions. 18mo.	30
The above two bound in 1 vol.	50
Newton's (Rev. John) Works. Comprising his Life, Letters, Hymns, Sermons, &c. 2 vols., 8vo.	3 00
Life. Separate. 18mo.	30
Noel's Infant Piety. 18mo.	25
North American Indians. Illustrated. 18mo.	50
Olmsted's Thoughts and Counsels for the Impenitent.	50
Old White Meeting-House. 18mo.	40
Owen on Spiritual Mindedness. 12mo.	60
Old Humphrey's Observations; Addresses; Thoughts for the Thoughtful; Homely Hints; Walks in London; Country Strolls; Old Sea Captain; Grandparents; Isle of Wight; Pithy Papers; and Pleasant Tales. 11 vols. Each	40
Paley's Horæ Paulinæ. 12mo.	75
Paterson on the Assembly's Shorter Catechism. 18mo.	50
Pike's True Happiness. 18mo.	30
Religion and Eternal Life. 18mo.	30
Divine Origin of Christianity. 18mo.	30
Pike & Hayward's Cases of Conscience.	

Philip's Devotional Guides. 2 vols., 12mo. 1 50
Marys. 40
Marthas. 40
Lydias. 40
Hannahs. 40
Love of the Spirit. 40
Young Man's Closet Library.

Pollok's Course of Time, the most elegant edition ever published; printed on superfine paper. 16mo. With portrait. Cloth, 1 00
gilt cloth, extra, 1 50
Turkey morocco, gilt, 2 00
small copy, close type. 18mo. 40
Life, Letters, and Remains. By the Rev. James Scott, D.D. With portrait. 16mo. 1 00
——— gilt cloth, extra. 1 50
Tales of the Scottish Covenanters, printed on large paper, uniform with the above. With portrait, 75
Do, do. small copy, 18mo. 50
Helen of the Glen. 18mo. 25
Persecuted Family. 18mo. 25
Ralph Gemmell. 18mo. 25

Porteus' Lectures on Matthew. 12mo. 60
Retrospect (The), by Aliquis. 18mo. 40
Richmond's Annals of the Poor. 18mo. 40
Rogers' Jacob's Well. 18mo. 40
Romaine on Faith. 12mo. 60
Letters. 12mo. 60
Scott's Force of Truth. 18mo. 25
Scougal's Works. 18mo. 40
Select Works of James, Venn, Wilson, Philip, and Jay. Eight complete works in one volume. Royal 8vo. 1 50
Select Christian Anthors, comprising Doddridge, Wilberforce, Adams, Halyburton, à Kempis, &c. With Introductory Essays by Dr. Chalmers, Bishop Wilson, and others. 2 vols. 8vo. 2 00

Serle's Christian Remembrancer. 18mo.	50
Sinner's Friend. 18mo.	25
Sigourney (Mrs. L. H.) Water Drops. 16mo.	75
gilt, extra,	1 25
Sinclair's Hill and Valley. 12mo.	60
Charlie Seymour. 18mo.	30
Simeon's Life, by Carus; with an Introductory Essay by Bishop McIlvaine. With portrait. 8vo.	2 00
Sir Roland Ashton, a Tale of the Times. By Lady Catharine Long 12mo.	75
Smyth's Bereaved Parents Consoled. 12mo.	75
Sorrowing Yet Rejoicing. 18mo.	30
32mo. gilt,	30
Stevenson's Christ on the Cross. 12mo.	75
Lord our Shepherd. 12mo.	60
Sumner's Exposition of Matthew and Mark. 12mo.	75
Suddard's British Pulpit. 2 vols. 8vo.	3 00
Symington on the Atonement. 12mo.	75
on the Dominion. 12mo.	75
Tacitus' Works, translated. Edited by Murphy. 8vo.	
Tennent's Life. 18mo.	25
Tholuck's Circle of Human Life. 18mo.	30
Taylor's (Jane) Life and Correspondence. 18mo.	40
Contributions of Q. Q. 2 vols.	80
Original Poems. 18mo.	30
Display, a Tale. 18mo.	30
Mother and Daughter	30
Essays in Rhyme. 18mo.	30
Turretine's Complete Works, in the original Latin.	
The Theological Sketch Book, or Skeletons of Sermons, so arranged as to constitute a complete Body of Divinity. From Simeon, Hannam, Benson, &c. 2 vols.	3 00
Tyng's Lectures on the Law and Gospel. New edition, large type, with a fine portrait. 8vo.	1 50
Christ is All. 8vo. With portrait	1 50
Israel of God. 8vo.	

Tyng's Recollections of England. 12mo. 1 00
Thucydides' History of the Peloponnesian War. Translated by Wm. Smith. 8vo.
Turnbull's Genius of Scotland, or Sketches of Scottish Scenery, Literature, and Religion. 12mo. 1 00
Pulpit Orators of France and Switzerland, with Sketches of their Character, and Specimens of their Eloquence. With portrait of Fenelon, 12mo. 1 00
Waterbury's Book for the Sabbath. 18mo. 40
Whately's Kingdom of Christ and Errors of Romanism. 8vo. 75
Whitecross' Anecdotes on the Assembly's Catechism 30
White's Meditation on Prayer. 18mo. 40
Believer; a Series of Discourses. 18mo. 40
Practical Reflections on the Second Advent. 18mo. 40
Wilson's Lights and Shadows of Scottish Life. 18mo. 50
Winslow on Personal Declension and Revival, 60
Wylie's Journey over the Region of Fulfilled Prophecy. 30
Xenophon's Whole Works. Translated by Cooper, Spelman, Smith, Fielding, and others. 8vo.

www.ingramcontent.com/pod-product-compliance
Lightning Source LLC
LaVergne TN
LVHW010208110826
845151LV00002B/636

* 9 7 8 1 4 2 5 5 3 6 0 2 2 *